Becoming a Whole Person in a Broken World

Discovery House
P U B L I S H E R S
BOX 3566 · GRAND RAPIDS, MI 49501

*PUBLISHING BOOKS THAT FEED
THE SOUL WITH THE WORD OF GOD.*

BECOMING
A WHOLE
PERSON
IN A
BROKEN
WORLD

Studies in the Book of Romans

by

Ron Lee Davis

with

James D. Denney

Some names, places, and events in this book
have been altered to protect the privacy
of the individuals involved.

Becoming a Whole Person in a Broken World
Copyright © 1990 by Ron Lee Davis

Unless indicated otherwise, Scripture is taken from the
HOLY BIBLE, NEW INTERNATIONAL VERSION.
Copyright © 1973, 1978, 1984 International Bible Society.
Used by permission of Zondervan Bible Publishers.

Library of Congress Cataloging-in-Publication Data

Davis, Ron Lee.
Becoming a whole person in a broken world:
studies in the book of Romans/
by Ron Lee Davis with James D. Denney
p. cm.
Includes bibliographical references.

ISBN 0-929239-29-6

1. Bible. N.T. Romans—Devotional literature.
I. Denney James D. II. Title
BS2665.4.D33 1990 227'.107—dc20 90-41358
CIP

Discovery House Publishers is affiliated with Radio Bible Class,
Grand Rapids, Michigan

Printed in the United States of America

90 91 92 93 94 / CHG / 10 9 8 7 6 5 4 3 2

Lovingly dedicated
to the people of
the Westminster Presbyterian Church
of Clarinda, Iowa,
with many fond memories
and deep affection.

Also by RON LEE DAVIS:

Gold in the Making

A Forgiving God in an Unforgiving World

Healing Life's Hurts

A Time for Compassion

Courage to Begin Again

Mistreated

CONTENTS

INTRODUCTION

A Love Letter From God

My friend Don Kingsborough is an American success story. He first became a corporate heavy-hitter as president of Atari, then as the man who brought Nintendo to America, and most recently as the founder of Worlds of Wonder, the fastest-growing American corporation of the late 1980s. Don was the genius behind the famous talking bear Teddy Ruxpin and the electronic adventure game Laser Tag.

He has been profiled and interviewed on *Good Morning America*, *The Today Show*, *Dick Cavett*, *The Tonight Show* with Johnny Carson, and ABC's *20/20*. Cover stories and feature articles in *Business World*, *Fortune*, and *People* have chronicled his career. But recently, Don shared with me a side of his story the reporters never covered.

"Though my career has been focused on developing and marketing games and gadgets for children," he told me, "my own childhood was very unhappy. My most vivid early memory is one of desperately wanting to escape from my family. That's painful to admit, but true. I just wanted to grow up and leave home at the earliest possible moment."

Don was the youngest of seven children. Neither of his parents had more than a third grade education, and none of his brothers or sisters ever graduated from high school. His family had moved from Oklahoma to California during the Dust Bowl years. They settled in a federal housing project in Richmond, an industrial port city north of Oakland, and Don's father, brothers, and sisters all got jobs in the same factory.

"Every day at five o'clock," Don explained, "we all came together for dinner. Even after my brothers and sisters started their own families and moved out, they still came home for dinner on the weekend. Yet, there was no real closeness at all. There was nothing emotionally or spiritually to hold our family together— no joy, no common bond. We were just a collection of isolated people."

Don related to me one starkly etched memory he still carries from childhood. "I was about eight years old," he said. "It was a Friday evening and I was coming downstairs from my bedroom. I got to the bottom of the stairs, turned the corner, and looked into the living room. There was my entire family—my mother and father, my three sisters and two brothers, and some of their children. The room was smoky and lit only by the flickering TV screen. My parents, my brothers, and my sisters were all smoking cigarettes and watching the fights, which was the big Friday-night thing on TV back then. An air of loneliness and meaninglessness hung over my family. Even as an eight-year-old child I felt the oppression of the awful emptiness of their lives.

"I turned and ran up the stairs to my room. I had a terrible sensation in my chest, more intense than sadness or depression. I think it was really fear—fear so great it was like a physical revulsion. I was afraid of being locked into the kind of future I had just seen, afraid of that horrible emptiness. I wanted to scream, 'I can't live here! Let me out of here!'

"At that moment, I knew I had to change the course of

my life. I knew that to live as my family lived would be the same as death. So I set my sights on a word that has driven me ever since: *success*."

Through grade school, high school, and college, Don was haunted by the image of his family enveloped in cigarette smoke, loneliness, and futility. This image stoked his determination to excel, and propelled him toward his goal of success. He pressed toward his goal with a single-mindedness that bordered on ferocity.

As Don grew older, he filled his mind with motivational slogans: "Destiny is not a matter of chance, but of choice." "Genius is one percent inspiration and ninety-nine percent perspiration." "Things may come to those who wait, but only the things left over from those who hustle."

Don had never been to church or Sunday school. His only exposure to God was a college philosophy course that derided Christianity as a myth. People who believed in Jesus Christ, Don thought, simply used their faith as a crutch. The idea of a loving God was not even a subject for intelligent discussion.

Don entered the business world just as Silicon Valley— a center of high-tech industry south of San Francisco— was coming into existence. Throughout this area, new ideas, technologies, and companies were springing up weekly. Money flowed like water through this electrifying community.

Don Kingsborough got in on the ground floor of an innovative consumer electronics company as vice president of sales and marketing. This company, starting with only a few thousand dollars and a handful of employees, soon grew to become a $2.5 billion giant. The company was called Atari.

"Every day was an adventure," Don recalls. "Concentrated in this one little corner of California were the best minds and most innovative companies in the world. We were creating a whole new world with human ingenuity and silicon chips. Every few weeks brought some astounding revolution in the industry. The excitement was like a drug."

Don met his wife, Rebecca, at this time. To him, marriage was a logical decision, a good career move. People around him were getting married, because marriage added to the stable image most top executives want to project. A dazzling conversationalist and an attractive companion at cocktail parties, Rebecca was an asset to Don's prestige.

But Rebecca had some unsettling ideas. She talked a lot about God. She told Don that Jesus died for his sin, and if he would believe in Jesus he would have everlasting life. Don had no use for such ideas as God, sin, forgiveness, or heaven. "The things Rebecca talked about made no sense to me," he said. "So after a while, I just tuned out. If Rebecca wanted to believe that stuff, I figured it was harmless."

Don's career skyrocketed. He moved from vice president to the top slot in Atari, commanding a six-figure income. He flew in a $20 million company jet. A limousine with all the amenities took him anywhere he wanted to go, including the finest restaurants. He had a beautiful wife, three handsome children, a luxurious home—the realization of the American dream. He had achieved the lifestyle he craved as a boy. He was a *success*.

Yet he was empty. He was lonely. His life had no meaning. "There were times," he said, "when I was sitting in that corporate jet or in our expensive home, and I would still be haunted by the image of loneliness and emptiness from my childhood. I could go to Europe or the finest night spots in New York, but wherever I went, the emptiness went with me. I tried to fill the emptiness with material things. But with all I had, what does one more Mercedes mean? So then I tried to fill the emptiness in other ways. And that destroyed my marriage." Leaving the wreckage of his marriage behind, he moved to Palo Alto.

One Monday night, he came home tired from working through the weekend. He put a frozen dinner in the oven and switched the TV on. He ate while watching a football game, and fell asleep on the sofa before halftime. He awoke just before the game was over and dragged himself to bed. With the covers pulled up to his neck, he noticed a strange sensation. He felt one muscle stiffen rock-hard, then another, then another. Paralysis crept over him like an infection, muscle after muscle turning to stone. Finally, he felt as though he were carved from cold marble, aware yet numb and rigid.

His eyes snapped open. He sat bolt upright. His pulse raced with the thrill of fear. Had he been asleep? Was it just a dream? It seemed so real!

He got no more sleep that night.

The next morning, Don contemplated his strange, troubling dream—if it was a dream. Haggard and pale, wearying of all the comments on how tired he looked, he somehow made it through the day. Returning home that night, feeling not only tired but a little ill, he went immediately to bed. Moments later, he noticed a familiar sensation. One muscle stiffened, then another. Soon his entire body had turned to stone.

He sat up, his face filmed with cold sweat. "What's happening?" he wondered. "Am I sick? What's wrong with me?" Again, he got no sleep.

The next night came. For the first time since childhood, Don was afraid to sleep. He lay in bed, waiting. Again, that strange sensation as, one by one, his muscles turned to stone. When two-thirds of his body had become paralyzed, he heard the Voice. It was not like someone speaking in the room. It was a voice within. As it spoke to him, a ray of light appeared from nowhere, shining on the wall opposite him.

He answered the Voice. Later, he was never sure whether his conversation lasted five minutes or an hour, yet he remembered the content of the conversation in detail. It was all about *him*, about everything that had ever happened in his life. The voice walked him through his memories—memories of hurts he had received and hurts he had caused others, especially Rebecca and the children. He suddenly understood all the things in his life he had done badly, and all he had done right. Most important, he knew exactly how he should live the rest of his life.

Don climbed out of bed and went to his knees. Though he had never prayed before, even as a child, he poured out his heart to Jesus. "I knew I had to ask Jesus to forgive me," Don later recalled. "I asked Him to live through me and set my life straight." Then he was able to sleep.

The next evening, Don went to Rebecca and told her everything. "I know what has to happen now," he told her. "We have to spend the rest of our lives together. I love you, and our family needs to be together."

Rebecca didn't believe him. Don's story was too

fantastic. It took him a week of visits and phone calls to convince her of his sincerity. But finally she consented to marry Don again. Today, their marriage is a testimony to the transforming power of Jesus Christ. Don's relationship with Rebecca and his children is stronger than he could have imagined. The emptiness that once haunted him has been filled with meaning and love—the love of Jesus Christ and the love of his family.

That ending might seem happy enough, but Don's story goes on. His walk with Jesus has grown deeper every day. Those who knew Don before his encounter with Jesus Christ have marked a profound change in him. His Christian faith now pervades every dimension of his life, both personal and professional.

Does that mean success is no longer important to Don Kingsborough? "No, I still want to be a success," he replies. "I recently founded a new company, and I want it to be successful. But my definition of success has changed. Today, I define success as having a close relationship with Jesus Christ. I didn't know it at the time, but that's what I really wanted when I was a little boy growing up in Richmond. I was looking for God's love. Now I've found it. The emptiness is gone. I'm a whole human being."

Don Kingsborough has emerged from a world of brokenness and emptiness, and has been made whole by the love of Jesus Christ. He's a living demonstration of the power of God to transform lives, a power the apostle Paul describes for us in his blueprint for spiritual, emotional, and relational wholeness, the book of Romans. Paul writes, "I am not ashamed of the gospel, because it is the power of God for the salvation of everyone who believes" (Romans 1:16).

Paul's letter to the Christians in Rome is nothing less than a gospel of wholeness for today's broken world. Without question, it remains one of the most dynamic, timely, and applicable books in the Bible. Its energy arcs across the centuries and continues to electrify the hearts of men and women in the 1990s. Though the most theologically profound of Paul's letters, it is also rich in practical insight for our everyday lives. Is there suffering in your life? Paul's strategy for suffering is in Romans 5. Do you need strength to face temptation? Study Romans 6, 7, and 8. Wrestling with guilt and fear of punishment? Romans 3, 4, and 5 will comfort and refresh you. Confused about spiritual gifts? Feeling lonely and isolated? Feeling angry and resentful because someone has mistreated you? Turn to Romans 12 for counsel and insight.

As you read through Romans, there will be times when you feel you're in touch with the wisdom of the ages, and other times when Paul's message will be so direct and contemporary you may wonder if the ink of the pages has had time to dry. The emotional content of this extraordinary letter is compelling, dynamic, shifting in mood from page to page. Paul is by turns stern and confrontational, passionate and persuasive, comforting and affectionate, or as understanding as an old friend.

Over the years, I have led three different congregations through this remarkable book, and during each message series in Romans two things have happened: (1) I discovered powerful new truths that have deepened my relationship with God, and (2) friends in each congregation have asked me to write a book on Romans. At last, the book has been written, yet I want to point out that this book is not a collection of sermons in book form. Rather, in the process of writing this book I have tried yet again to approach the book of Romans from a fresh vantage, seeking new and meaningful insights for the changing world of the 1990s.

Dwight L. Moody once observed that Scripture was not given to increase our knowledge but to change our lives. And I can testify that my own process of discovery and application of the truths of Romans has had a transforming effect upon my own life. My prayer, as you study along with me in the power-filled lines of Paul's letter to the Romans, is that you will experience the same transforming effect upon your own life. In the book of Romans we will discover:

- the most important goal in the Christian life;
- how to authentically *rejoice*, even in suffering;
- how to experience the energizing presence of God's Spirit;
- how we can uphold the *truth* of God while projecting the *mercy* of God in an age of moral anarchy, sexual confusion, pornography, and AIDS;
- how to tell the difference between wise discernment and self-righteous judgment;
- how to find strength to face the life-long struggle against temptation and sin;
- how to maintain a clear Christian witness in a time of New Age heresies and greedy materialism;
- how to discover and use your spiritual gifts; and
- how to live out genuine Christian love in the trenches of everyday life.

This book is not a technical verse-by-verse commentary on Romans. Rather, we focus on the major themes that intimately affect us as we live out our faith in an increasingly hostile and anti-Christian world. Our goal is to discover the truths in this amazing document that have special relevance to our lives. So I invite you to keep a Bible open alongside this book while prayerfully opening your heart to the new insights God wants to pour out from His Word.

But let me warn you: The first few pages of Romans are strong stuff. Romans is sort of a good-news/bad-news proposition, and Paul gives us the bad news first. The bad news is that we are all sinners, we are under God's judgment, and we are helpless in our own strength to erase the guilt and sin from our lives. Paul relentlessly drives the bad news home from chapter 1 through the first half of chapter 3: All have sinned and fallen short of the glory of God, no exceptions, none, period.

Now, are you ready for the good news? Actually, to merely call Paul's message in Romans "good news" would be the understatement of the last two millenniums! The message of Romans is ultimately the *best* news we could ever hear: God has seen you and me at our worst, and yet His first words to us are "I love you." Paul's message is an exhilarating message of freedom and wholeness for you and me.

Arnold Parker tells a story that's a parable of Paul's good news in Romans. It's the story of Hulda, a nurse who worked in a European hospital in the 1950s. One Sunday Hulda was leaving church when she was stopped by her pastor. "Hulda," he said, "what's happened to you? Where did you get all those bruises and scratches?"

"They're nothing, really, pastor," Hulda replied shyly. "They'll heal in a few days."

Hulda's evasive answer only fueled the pastor's

curiosity and concern, so he went to one of Hulda's co-workers to find out the cause of her wounds. The co-worker told him the following story:

Two weeks earlier, a fourteen-year-old girl was brought to the hospital, uncontrollable and violently insane. Raised in poverty, the child of abusive, alcoholic parents, this little girl had never known love or any sense of belonging. At age twelve, she watched as her parents wrestled over a gun. During the struggle, the gun discharged, killing her father. The memory of the blood and the sound of his dying moans drenched her nightmares. Her mother avoided prison by pleading self-defense and persuading the court that her little girl needed a mother's care. Yet the only "care" this girl received from her mother was the same she had always received: beatings, curses, rejection.

Finally something snapped inside this child. She had become so filled with pain and hatred of her life that she completely rejected reality. Yet the fantasy-life to which she retreated seemed just as violent as the reality she had fled. She thrashed and clawed at everyone around her, screaming incoherently. Her eyes were wild and devoid of human emotion.

The physician in charge decided the only therapy that could help the child was a method called *catharsis*, which was in fairly common use in those days. *Catharsis* literally means a purging of poisonous emotions. "To be healed," said the doctor to his staff, "the girl must be allowed to vent her rage on someone. I don't have to tell you what this means. I'm asking for a volunteer."

Only one hand went up. Hulda's.

Every day for the next two weeks, Hulda allowed herself to be placed in a cell with the girl for a full hour of continuous assault. The girl kicked, clawed, and pummeled Hulda until all her strength was spent. Then she collapsed in a huddle, trembling like a frightened, trapped animal in one corner of the room.

After each assault, Hulda would bend down to the girl while trickles of her own blood ran down her face and arms. Again and again she repeated, "Darling, I love you." Hulda subjected herself to this ordeal day after day, until a subtle change came over the girl. The violence and hatred began seeping out of her, and she gradually responded to Hulda's self-sacrificing love with tears and affection. She was becoming whole again.

Hulda's costly love for this fourteen-year-old girl is a beautiful parable of God's love for us, exemplified by the sacrifice of Jesus Christ on the cross. Even while we rebelled against Him, cursed Him, and drove nails into His flesh, He was saying to us, "I love you." The good news of Romans is that God has seen us at our worst—and He still loves us.

So turn the page, and together let's explore this amazing, challenging, encouraging love letter from God . . .

Chapter 1

The Gospel of Wholeness

(An Overview)

For my friend Paul Mullins, this would be one of the hardest days of his life. While driving to the office of the advertising agency he operated in central California, Paul was thinking not about business, but about his father. It was only the day before, as he and his family were arriving home from church, that the phone had rung with the bad news: Paul's father had collapsed and died of a heart attack while teaching Sunday school. Now, on this gray Monday morning, Paul was going to the office to tie up some loose ends before driving to southern California for the funeral.

He parked the car and walked to the door of the office, pondering the fact that the pressures and deadlines that had seemed so important on Friday meant so little to him on this Monday. As he turned the key and opened the door, Paul heard an outburst of profanity behind him. He turned and saw a young man in blue jeans, about nineteen years old, stamping up the sidewalk toward him, his face twisted in rage. Paul thought, *Is this guy mad at me?* But then he noticed the young man's car sitting by the curb with a flat tire. The stream of the stranger's unprintable tirade against his car continued until he was just a few steps away from Paul.

"Can I help you?" said Paul.

"I need to use a phone," the young man answered, without any noticeable cordiality or gratitude.

"Sure," said Paul, holding the door for him. "It's there on the desk."

"Why does everything happen to me?" the fellow said, picking up the phone and dialing. "My Dad's gonna kill me!" Remembering his own Dad, Paul felt like saying, *I'd gladly trade problems with you, my friend*. The young man made his call, shouting and swearing at someone on the other end.

"You know, Ron," Paul later told me, "I've often thought about that fellow whenever I've had a rough day at work or some little thing has gone wrong around the house. People fall completely apart over the littlest things, yet most of our problems just don't stack up to the eternal issues—how we live, how we die, how we show our love for each other. I was feeling a lot of hurt that day. Even though I knew my Dad was with the Lord, I really missed him. But though the hurt was there, the Lord was with me, too. I don't think I could have handled that day without Christ."

Two very different orders of trial and disappointment. Two totally different responses. The young man who responded to a flat tire with anger and a steady stream of profanity is symptomatic of so many people in this age of ours—people with brittle spirits, easily broken by this world and its troubles. A mere mechanical annoyance completely destroyed his composure, sending him into a tailspin of hostility, self-pity, and offensive language.

My friend, Paul, however, was demonstrating what it means to be a whole person in a broken world. Amid the pain he felt, there was peace. Though Paul's world was broken by grief, he himself was not broken by despair. He was whole in spirit, whole in faith. He was a living example of the words written almost two thousand years ago by another man named Paul: "Do not conform any longer to the pattern of this world, but be transformed by the renewing of your mind" (Romans 12:2).

As we begin our journey through the book of Romans, we should place this document in its cultural and historical context. The world of the apostle Paul was a *broken* world, full of misery, immorality, and injustice. The world was under the heel of Rome, and the Roman empire was ruled by Nero, a cruel and insane king. Nero was known not only for his political treachery, but for his gross sexual immorality. The Roman historian Tacitus, in *The Annals*, observed, "Nero, who polluted himself by every lawful or lawless indulgence, had not omitted a single abomination which could heighten his depravity."[1] Tacitus went on to describe Nero's sins, but the details are too loathsome to repeat here.

Even more appalling than Nero's obscene debaucheries was his sadistic persecution of the early Christian church. Nero had invented his own religion out of bits and pieces of pagan mystery-religions and magical systems. For the followers of Jesus Christ, he had nothing but hatred. Tacitus wrote, "Nero . . . inflicted the most exquisite tortures on a class . . . called Christians . . . . Mockery of every sort was added to their deaths. Covered with the skins of beasts, they were torn by dogs and perished, or were nailed to crosses, or were doomed to the flames."[2] In fact, hundreds of Christians were covered with pitch, hung on poles, and burned alive as torches in Nero's garden.

This was the world the apostle Paul strode—a bloody, perilous, cruel world. And yet it was just such a broken world that God, through his servant Paul, chose to penetrate with a new manifesto, a new gospel of wholeness.

Paul's letter to the Christians in Rome is actually a kind of "fifth gospel." Whereas the gospels of Matthew, Mark, Luke, and John bear witness to the life, death, and resurrection of Jesus, the gospel of Romans bears witness to the *life-changing* power of Jesus. Moreover, Paul writes Romans with the authority of experience, for his own life had in fact been radically transformed by an encounter with Jesus Christ.

Before his transformation, Paul was a man who hated Christ, Christianity, and Christians. He was a proud Jewish rabbi who traced his lineage back to King David. He was also a member of the rigidly orthodox Jewish sect called the Pharisees. He had set before himself the goal of completely exterminating the Christian faith from the earth.

Acts 9 records the story of Paul's high-voltage encounter with Jesus. He was on the road to Damascus, traveling on yet another mission to find and arrest Christians, when he was suddenly struck down by a blinding vision from heaven. In this encounter he heard, saw, and spoke with the risen Christ, and from that day forward the entire course of his life was turned in a totally new direction.

Paul became a missionary, going throughout the Roman world preaching the gospel of Jesus Christ, making converts, founding new churches, and writing letters of encouragement and counsel to those churches. One such letter was Paul's letter to the Christians in Rome, which he wrote from the Greek city of Corinth sometime in the winter of A.D. 56 or 57. One fact that becomes clear as we read through Romans is that Paul is uniquely equipped to communicate the gospel to both Jewish and non-Jewish listeners, because he had been raised and educated in the rich traditions of both Greek philosophy and the Jewish faith. He was a Roman citizen, but in terms of his education and his outlook, he was truly a citizen of the world.

The message of Romans is rousing and compelling. It burns with urgency. The dramatic power of Paul's letter speaks to every culture, every age, from Paul's own time to our fast-paced era of the 1990s. The sixteenth-century Swiss reformer John Calvin wrote, "When anyone gains a knowledge of this letter, he has an entrance to all the hidden treasures of Scripture." The poet Samuel Taylor Coleridge called Romans "the most profound work in existence." F. F. Bruce, the insightful Bible commentator, noted that Romans has "liberated the minds of men, brought them back to an understanding of the essential Gospel of Christ, and started spiritual revolutions." Earl Palmer, in *Salvation by Surprise*, said, "The letter to the Romans is Paul's major work. It has challenged Christians through the centuries and has played a key role in each of the great periods of renewal and reformation of the church."[3]

Whenever and wherever the message of Romans is eagerly received, startling events take place. Hearts are changed. Spiritual revivals explode. Whole churches, cities, and institutions are rocked on their foundations.

The message of Romans is a message of transformation and healing for a broken and dying world.

Three centuries after the writing of Romans, there lived a North African Roman named Augustine. Like Paul's world in the first century, Augustine's world was a broken world. The Roman empire was crumbling under assault from the Vandals to the south and the Goths to the north. Political turmoil and religious wars filled people everywhere with fear. The deceptive cult of Manichaeism struggled with the early Christian church in a fierce rivalry for the hearts of men and women—and for a while it appeared that authentic Christianity was losing. In fact, Augustine himself had been seduced by this heretical cult.

In his autobiography, *The Confessions*, Augustine describes the intense spiritual war that raged within him when he was a young man. The doctrines and practices of the Manichaean cult had begun to seem hollow to him, for Manichaeism taught that people needed no Savior, but were perfected by knowledge alone. Recognizing at last that he was powerless to live a sinless life by his own power, he was relentlessly haunted by the memory of past sins. "I was tossed about, and wasted, and dissipated," he wrote, "and I boiled over in my fornications."[4]

During this time of spiritual anguish, he went out into his garden with his friend Alypius. He took with him a hand-copied volume of Romans given him by his devoutly Christian mother. As he sat down beneath a fig tree a few paces from his friend, the book slipped from his fingers and fell into the grass. Augustine wept bitterly for his lost soul, certain that his sins were beyond forgiveness. And while he poured out his tears, an unusual thing happened. From over the hedge of the garden, Augustine heard a child's voice chanting, "Take up and read; take up and read." Seeing the book at his feet, Augustine felt that God was using the child to speak to him.[5]

Augustine picked up the book of Romans, opened it, and began reading. In those moments, his life was forever changed. Suddenly he understood not only the crisis of his sin but its solution in Jesus Christ. After he finished reading, he rushed to his friend Alypius and shared the life-changing message of Romans with him. Alypius became not only Augustine's first convert, but the first among thousands to be touched by the teaching and writing ministry of this man whom history now remembers as St. Augustine, Bishop of Hippo.

Like the fourth century world of Augustine, the sixteenth-century world of Martin Luther was a broken world. The Christian church had hardened into an institution with enormous wealth and worldly power. Instead of offering salvation by the preaching of God's Word, the corrupt institutional church had begun selling salvation and other spiritual privileges for money in the form of so-called "indulgences." The church had also become involved in political intrigues and manipulation of European governments. The richer and more powerful it became, the more spiritually and morally bankrupt it became.

Yet, in one small corner of this huge religious machine, Martin Luther labored to communicate the truth of the Bible to the simple people of his parish church. He was a young man, not more than thirty-five years old, yet he was a man of deep conviction. While he was preparing a series of sermons from Romans,

Luther discovered a statement that the institutional church had long ago ceased to teach or practice: ". . . righteousness from God comes through faith in Jesus Christ to all who believe . . ." (Romans 3:22). That verse suddenly leaped out at him like a startling new revelation. "Thereupon I felt myself to be reborn," he later wrote, "and to have entered through open doors into paradise."

Energized by this dynamic insight into spiritual reality, Luther took a bold stand against the corrupt church institution. With Romans as his authority, Luther proclaimed that men and women are justified by grace through faith in Jesus Christ alone—and his proclamation set off a chain reaction of renewal and revival that spread around the world: the Protestant Reformation.

Like Luther's world, eighteenth-century England was a broken world of rampant unemployment, homelessness, debtor's prisons, hunger, disease, and illiteracy. These dire social problems weighed heavily on a young London clergyman named John Wesley, director of a relief agency called Holy Club. Working long, strenuous hours every day, he visited prisons, poorhouses, and workhouses, distributing food, clothes, and medicines, while at the same time running a school for the poor. At the end of five years, he had worked himself into complete exhaustion and had to resign from Holy Club. Without his energy and drive, the organization quickly collapsed.

Seeing himself as a failure, Wesley boarded a ship for America to begin a new life as a missionary to American Indians in the Colony of Georgia. Again, he fell into his old patterns of workaholism and exhaustion. He had no sense of God's peace or contentment. He fell in love with a woman, but she spurned him and married another man. The people with whom he ministered grew dissatisfied with his leadership and began to openly oppose him. Feeling his whole world again crumbling around him, Wesley returned to England in defeat.

On May 24, 1738, this dejected young man stood in a crowd at an outdoor evangelistic meeting in Aldersgate Street, London. On the wooden platform, a preacher stood and read from Martin Luther's preface to the book of Romans. There, for the first time, John Wesley grasped a truth from Romans that had eluded him throughout his years of ministry: *Salvation is by grace through faith alone.* Wesley later recalled, "My heart was strangely warmed. I trusted in Christ alone for salvation, and received the assurance that he had taken away my sins and saved me from the law of sin and death."

Suddenly, Wesley had a new reason to serve God and humanity. His intellectual religion had been transformed into a profoundly personal *relationship* with the living God. From that day forward, this young man (he was in his mid-thirties at the time of his Aldersgate experience) traveled all over England, preaching the good news of Jesus Christ. He organized small groups of believers who prayed and studied Scripture together, who confessed their hurts, struggles, and sins to one another, and who were accountable and committed to one another.

Energized by an amazing inner power, Wesley seemed as active as he had been in his earlier years, yet without his old symptoms of burnout and failure. The gospel he preached—a gospel rooted in the book of Romans—was picked up and expounded by other preachers, such as George Whitefield. Revival and renewal spread like wildfire, first throughout England, and then across the ocean to America.

Like the world of Paul, of Augustine, of Luther, of Wesley, our own world is a place of tragic brokenness. Every time we open the newspaper or turn on the television we're confronted with nuclear anxiety, moral anarchy, ethical emptiness, race hatred, abortion, pollution, famine, poverty, AIDS, terrorism, drugs, and crime. If we dare to honestly examine our rosy-tinted illusion of modern social progress, we are forced to admit that ours is actually the bloodiest century in human history. No other century has seen war, famine, suffering, and mass extermination on the scale our age has produced.

Amazingly, Paul's letter to the Romans—far from being irrelevant in such times—has actually proved all the more urgent and applicable in our era. The gospel of wholeness has never been more needed than it is here and now, in our broken world. My prayer, as you and I examine together the challenging truths of Romans, is that this powerful document will work its transforming miracle again in our own time. Just as the book of Romans has changed the course of previous generations, I pray its truths will spring forth in your life and mine to breathe a new fragrance of revival into our own generation.

*   *   *

As we step back and gain an overview of the structure of Romans, we see that Paul begins by confronting the whole human race. He indicts us all as utterly lost in sin. In fact, he presents our human sinfulness as an urgent crisis.

But Paul does not end on that negative note. He goes on to give us the solution to our crisis of sin. Paul's solution is a *Person*, Jesus Christ, sent from God to radically intervene in human history.

The letter to the Romans may be outlined as follows:
1. Paul Prosecutes Humankind   *Romans 1:1–3:20*
2. Paul Defends Humankind   *Romans 3:21–5:21*
3. A Strategy for Christian Living   *Romans 6–8*
4. Jesus and the Nation of Israel   *Romans 9–11*
5. Jesus and the Church   *Romans 12–16*

In the first section, Romans 1:1 to 3:20, Paul assumes the role of prosecutor in a courtroom of moral law. As we read this section, it's not hard to visualize this scene. You and I sit at the defendant's table, without even an attorney at our side. Before us, Paul strides the floor of the courtroom, eloquently building an iron-clad case of our guilt before the eternal Judge. We sink lower and lower into our chairs beneath the withering blast of Paul's brilliant prosecution of the case against us.

Paul begins in chapter 1 by talking in an impersonal way of people we like to think of as "those sinners over there," the pagans, the hedonists, the idolators, the immoral people of this world. They are the ones we feel smugly superior to: ". . . *they* exchanged the truth of God for a lie . . . *they* have become filled with every kind of wickedness, evil, greed and depravity . . . *they* are senseless, faithless, heartless, ruthless . . . ." We think, "Yes, *they* deserve condemnation. Yes, Paul, yes! Give it to them with both barrels!" And Paul does. But he doesn't stop there.

In chapter 2, Paul the Prosecutor goes on from *they* to *you*—the moral person, the good humanist, the person who sees himself as "okay" on the basis of his own good works: "*You* therefore, have no excuse, *you* who pass judgment on someone else . . . ."

In chapter 3, he moves from *you* to *we*, addressing the sin and guilt of the "religious" man or woman, the pious Jew of the first century, and the active church-goer of our own century, the one who says, "Oh, there's nothing wrong with me. I'm a very religious person." Even this person stands condemned by Paul the prosecutor. "Are *we* any better?" asks Paul in 3:9. "Not at all! *We* have already made the charge that Jews and Gentiles alike are all under sin."

But Paul is still not through. In one agonizing sentence Paul moves from *we* to *I*. "Why am I still condemned as a sinner?" he asks in 3:7. Passionately, persuasively, the apostle Paul has netted us all in, so that finally no one stands guiltless, no one has any shred of defense in the human crisis of sin, not even Prosecutor Paul himself!

Then in Romans 3:21, Paul does something amazing. He sheds his prosecutor's robes, stalks across the courtroom of human history, takes his place at the defendant's table—alongside you and me—and he begins to plead our case! "But now," he says, "a righteousness from God, apart from law, has been made known . . . ." The prosecutor has now become our defense attorney! And with the same impassioned eloquence, Paul begins to expound before us the good news that there is a solution to the human crisis of sin.

The solution is the revelation of God in Jesus Christ, who comes and teaches us how to live, who shows us how to love, who conquers death by disarming it on the cross, who is here with us, filling us with His resurrection power. The revelation of God in Jesus

Christ is the central event of all human history and it is sketched in for us in Romans 3:21–5:21. That revelation climaxes in 5:20, as Paul declares, "Where sin increased"—that's a reference to the "guilty" verdict of Romans 1:1–3:20—"grace increased all the more." That's the good news of Romans 3–5.

In chapters 6 through 8, Paul gives us God's strategy for Christian living. In this very well-organized and thoughtful document, he anticipates the question that naturally occurs to us: "All right, Paul, *if* I accept your assessment of my condition as a crisis of sin and guilt, and *if* I yield myself to Jesus Christ as the solution to that crisis, then what? How should I then live?"

Paul's answer in these chapters is an intensely personal, vulnerable, and autobiographical answer. He talks about the wonderful freedom we have as followers of Jesus Christ—and he also illuminates our struggle as Christians. "What I want to do I do not do, but what I hate I do" (Romans 7:15); that is the struggle from which there is no escape, the struggle that will haunt us all our days. Then, in chapter 8, Paul introduces us to the Holy Spirit. In fact, there are twenty references to the Holy Spirit in this one chapter, and the good news of Romans 8 is that the Spirit of God has come to aid us in our lifelong struggle against sin.

In chapters 9 through 11, Paul inserts a parenthesis, an interlude, because Paul knows he must address the special situation of the Jewish readers of this letter. So, in these chapters, Paul deals with such questions as: How does the revelation of God in Jesus Christ affect the nation of Israel? Are the Jews automatically redeemed by their heritage, or do they also need to receive Christ?

Finally, in chapters 12 through 16, in one of the most beautiful yet most overlooked sections of Romans, we see how Jesus is dynamically active in the life of the church. Whereas the first eleven chapters of Romans have been largely theological in tone, these last five chapters take on a distinctly pastoral, practical, and even intimate tone. Here, Paul addresses the day-to-day joys and irritations of rubbing elbows with other Christians in a close-knit fellowship. In the concluding chapters of Romans, you and I will learn what it truly means to love one another in the body of Christ.

This, then, is Scripture's "fifth gospel," a gospel of transformation, a gospel of wholeness for a broken world. As we begin our journey of discovery in Romans, let me share with you the story of a four-year-old boy who accidentally discovered one of the deep truths of Romans in his father's newspaper.

"Daddy!" the boy called out as he scampered into the living room and leaped into his father's lap. Waving a Nerf foam-football in his father's face, he yelped, "Play football with me, Daddy!"

"Oh, son, I'm too tired to play," he began. But then he was struck by an inspiration. "Son, I have a *great* idea!" The newspaper page he held in his hand featured a large photo of the earth as seen from space. He tore the page in pieces and handed the strips of torn paper to his son. The boy blinked back at his father, perplexed.

"Think of it as a puzzle, son," said the father. "Just take these pieces into your room and put the picture of the world back together with tape."

The boy looked at the strips of newspaper in one hand and the football in his other hand, then he looked dubiously back at his father.

"It'll be lots of fun," the father assured him. "Go on."

The boy shrugged and departed. The father settled back in his chair, certain he had won a good fifteen minutes of peace and quiet. He was wrong.

Two minutes later, the boy was back in the living room, holding up the newspaper page with the earth all neatly reassembled and taped together. The father was dumbfounded. "How did you do it so fast?" he asked.

"Easy," said the boy. He turned the page over. On the back was a picture of a man. "I just put the man together. When I did that, the world came together too."

And so it is with us. As we become people of wholeness, our broken world comes together too. My prayer, as we begin our study of Paul's gospel of wholeness, is that you and I become people of wholeness in this broken, hurting world. I pray that we become encouraged and empowered to make a transforming difference in the world around us.

Chapter 2

The Wrath
(Romans 1:1–18)

Calvin Coolidge, the thirtieth president of the United States, was nicknamed "Silent Cal" because of his famed tendency to economize on his words. A story is told about Coolidge's pre-White House days. It was a Sunday and he had gone to church alone while his wife lay in bed with a mild fever. When he returned home, Mrs. Coolidge asked, "How was the service, Calvin?"

"Fine."

"What did the preacher talk about?"

"Sin."

"And what did he say about sin?"

"He was against it."

As we begin our journey through Paul's letter to the Romans, we too could say with Coolidge-like understatement that God is against sin. The climax of this first section of Romans is verse 18: "The wrath of God is being revealed from heaven against all the godlessness and wickedness of men who suppress the truth by their wickedness." This is the crisis of humanity: All humankind is separated from God by sin. And as we examine the human crisis portrayed in Romans by the apostle Paul, we find ourselves wrestling with a question that has troubled Bible scholars through the ages: "What is the wrath of God?"

This was a question that baffled Martin Luther throughout his life. He once said, "I find God's love to be God's *own* work, but I find God's wrath to be God's *strange* work." I identify with the sentiments of Martin Luther. On a subjective, emotional level, I find the image of a loving, merciful God far more appealing than the image of a God of wrath. So do millions of other people. As a result, many have rejected the biblical concept of God's wrath. There are even many pastors who avoid teaching on the subject of wrath.

It's a difficult, unpopular topic, but it is an inextricable part of Paul's argument in the book of Romans. So you and I, in our desire to be faithful to the biblical text, will take an honest, unflinching look at the subject of God's wrath as it is portrayed in Romans 1.

Through the centuries, Bible scholars have puzzled over the "bad news" tone of Paul's opening argument. Why, they wonder, does Paul begin the masterpiece of all his letters in such a negative vein? Also puzzling is the tense in which Paul writes, "The wrath of God is being revealed . . . ." That's the continuous present tense, and it could just as well be translated, "The wrath of God is *continuously* being revealed . . . ." Paul is clearly telling us that the operation of God's wrath is continuous, ongoing, operating to the present day. What does Paul mean when he suggests that this wrath is operating continuously, even in our own time?

These are the kinds of questions I was asked a number of years ago in a letter from my friend, Ruth. In my book *A Forgiving God in an Unforgiving World*, I told Ruth's story, and it bears repeating here. Ruth was a young woman just seventeen years old, and she was attending a Christian conference on the East Coast where I was speaking. We talked together a few times during the conference, and it was clear she had many questions and doubts regarding God and the Bible. But it wasn't until a few weeks later, when I received a letter from her, that I learned how deeply painful and personal her questions were.

In her letter, she told me about a relationship that had recently ended between herself and a young man from England. He had come to America as an exchange student, and she had fallen in love with him. They were sexually involved with each other and Ruth became pregnant. The young man then lost interest in her and returned to England. Confused and afraid to seek counsel from her parents or her pastor, Ruth anxiously put off any decision. Finally, in the middle of her pregnancy, she decided to have an abortion. In her letter, she concluded:

> The problem, Dr. Davis, is that since I waited so long to make up my mind and get up enough nerve to have the abortion, there was some danger involved. I couldn't let my parents know about this, so I went ahead with it anyway. Now, because of that decision, I will be unable to have children in the future. I love children so much, and I've always wanted children of my own. Now I can't ever have them. I've ruined my chances. I just don't understand why God has put me through this.[1]

This is a deeply personal statement of a theological question that arises out of Romans 1:18. Ruth wants to know about the wrath of God, and she asks, "Why has God put me through this?" Her question might even be stated, "Why is God mad at me? Why is He hurting me?

Why is He punishing me this way?" As you are reading this, you might be thinking, "Ron, how can you be so presumptuous and judgmental? How can you say that this young woman's heartbreak is somehow attributable to the wrath of God?"

In reply, I would say that we must be clear on what the Bible teaches—and what it does *not* teach—about this difficult subject. First, I want you to know my own heart. I am, by nature, a grace-oriented person. It's much easier for me to indulge or excuse a fault in someone else than to confront it. And although there are certainly many stern, judgmental Christians around, I would say that the majority of Christians I've met tend, like me, to be grace-oriented people. The grace of God is appealing to us; the idea of God's wrath seems strange. We are baffled and even a little repelled by this concept.

Yet I believe much of the bafflement and repulsion inspired by this concept could be dispelled if we better understood what the Bible really means by *wrath*. For many, this word conjures an image of a God who looks upon us with suspicion, just waiting for us to sin. They think that as soon as we stumble, God reaches down and inflicts punishment. That's the image implied in Ruth's letter when she says, "I just don't understand why God has put me through this." She pictures a God who is angry with her, who wants to hurt her.

This image has been promoted by generations of preachers who have practiced a kind of "evangelistic terrorism." God has been pictured as a kind of cosmic ogre whom we dare not antagonize, and the "gospel" of such preachers has been, "If you don't give your life to Christ, you will incur the wrath of God!" Yet this "gospel" of fear is emphatically not the gospel of Romans.

To understand what Paul means when he talks about "wrath," we must first examine the word Paul uses. In the original Greek, Paul's word for "wrath" is *orge*, which has the sense of "God's holy aversion," his turning away from sin. I believe this is important because I'm convinced that the "wrath" Paul refers to is not a vengeful, personal anger but rather the impersonal moral order, the framework of moral laws God has created. Paul chose not to use the more personal and vivid term for "wrath," the Greek word *thermos*, a word which suggests heat, and from which we get such heat-related English words as *thermal*, *thermometer*, and *thermonuclear*. The Greek word *thermos* implies a hot, vindictive blast of violent anger. Inspired by the Holy Spirit, Paul chose instead a word that suggests that God has averted his eyes, has removed himself. It suggests an impersonal moral order rather than direct and vengeful retribution.

As we noted before, this verse is in the continuous present tense: The wrath of God is *continuously* being revealed. Again, this suggests the impersonal moral order at work. It is not a matter of some angry deity looking down from on high, waiting to squash us if we stray. Rather, there are moral laws that function in the moral universe, just as there are physical laws that function in the physical universe. We make choices, and there are consequences attached to those choices. It's a simple matter of cause and effect.

In many ways, "the wrath of God" as it is expressed in Romans may be viewed as the moral equivalent of the law of gravity. If we, in our God-given free will, attempt to defy the law of gravity by throwing ourselves off a tall building, we can hardly blame God and ask as we descend, "God, why are you dragging me down to the pavement? Why are you putting me through the terrible experience of this fall?" The operation of the law of gravity is simply part of the natural, impersonal order of the universe. You can ignore gravity, disagree with gravity, even rebel against gravity—but if you do so, you will have to pay a price. The same is true of God's moral laws.

The cause-and-effect consequences of sin are not a matter of God deliberately trying to punish us. *All* the punishment for our sin has been endured for us by Jesus on the cross, just as David assures us in Psalm 103:12, "As far as the east is from the west, so far has he removed our transgressions from us." But if we violate the laws of the impersonal moral order of the universe, there will be consequences—sometimes *tragic* consequences. God in His grace has tried to shield us from those consequences. Through His Word, He alerts us to the danger of ignoring His law. Through His Spirit, active in our conscience, He reminds us of the need to obey His moral law. Through the sacrifice of His Son, He removes the penalty of sin—eternal separation from Himself—so that we are free to live with joy. God is our Father, and He loves us with a fatherly love. He has no need or desire to "get even" with us; rather, He wants to *protect* us from the consequences of our poor choices.

This, in fact, is the message I wrote back to my young friend, Ruth. Her suffering was not a result of God's anger, but of God's impersonal moral order. God loves Ruth unconditionally, no matter what she has done. Even though the consequences of her choices are real and cannot be changed, God wants to use this trial to teach her about His transforming love and grace. Instead of changing her circumstances, she would have to allow those circumstances to *change her*, to make her more mature in Christ.

One of the poor choices I've made in my own life has been in the area of anxiety. Philippians 4:6 says, "Do not be anxious about anything, but in everything, by prayer and petition, with thanksgiving, present your requests to God." But I have been anxious over many things, and have often chosen to wrestle with my anxiety alone rather than present it to God in prayer. The Bible says, "Do not worry about tomorrow" (Matthew 6:34). But I have often worried and fretted over future events, loading my system unnecessarily with stress. The Bible says, "Cast all your anxiety on him because he cares for you" (1 Peter 5:7). But I have taken the burden of my cares and anxieties on myself. The result of these choices, which are in violation of God's moral order, is that I have suffered from time to time with physical disorders, for which I've had to undergo medical treatment.

When I have literally "worried myself sick" would I be justified in crying out, "God, why are you doing this to me?!" Of course not. The call of the gospel is a call to personal responsibility. We have been given free will, the ability to make choices. When our choices violate God's impersonal moral order, there are consequences. We incur the cause-and-effect moral law that Paul calls *wrath*.

Only three times in the entire New Testament do we find the phrase "the wrath of God." More frequently, we see the simple phrase, "the wrath"— again, conveying a sense of something impersonal, more like a force of nature than a personal, emotional fury. If you have been carrying around the image of an angry, vengeful God who is just waiting to punish you and take the joy out of your life, I want you to leave that false concept here forever. Never carry that idea with you again. Go and live out your Christian life with a new and biblically grounded image of God: a God of grace, a Father of love, holy and just, but merciful and protective.

Novelist Nikos Kazantzakis tells a parable about a poor man who lies dying in his little hovel. As his life slips away he thinks about all his past sins. As a young man, he remembers, he had been wild, hedonistic, and immoral. Now, in the final moments of his life, those old sins cling to him, making him feel dirty. He rubs his hands over his body, trying uselessly to remove the dirt of sin from his body. Then he dies.

As he enters heaven and comes into the presence of Jesus, he is still thinking about his sins, still rubbing his hands over his body, still feeling dirty all over. Jesus calls to him. He sees that Jesus has a basin of water and a sponge by him. Jesus dips the sponge into the water and washes all the dirt and sin off the man's body. He is clean.

But the man cannot accept the gift of complete cleansing Jesus gives him. Instead, he feels compelled to recite the list of all his sins to Jesus. As he is detailing them one by one, Jesus interrupts him. "Don't bother me with that now," says Jesus. "Go out and play."

That's grace. That's love. That's forgiveness. That's the way God deals with you and me—and with our sin, which has been cleansed by the saving work of Jesus Christ upon the cross.

A second misconception many of us have about

God's wrath is that God was a God of wrath in the Old Testament, but a God of grace in the New Testament. We falsely assume there was no grace in the Old Testament, nor wrath in the New. Nothing could be further from the truth. God is the same, yesterday, today, and always, and whenever the church has taught otherwise, it has been led into error and heresy.

One of the early heresies the fledgling Christian church had to fend off was that of the *demiurge*, the "god below God." The Gnostic cults of the third and fourth centuries A.D. preached that the Christian God was a jealous and inferior god who created the world with all its imperfections, and whom Christians worshiped in ignorance. The Gnostics saw themselves as having superior knowledge, worshiping a superior God who had succeeded the inferior *demiurge*, the God of wrath. The Gnostic heresy even began to encroach upon the thinking of the early church, but the church awoke in time and, guided by the truths of Romans, said, "No! There is only *one* God. He is holy and just, but He is also loving and gracious. Moreover, He is consistent, He is unchanging."

P. T. Forsythe says, "As you get an overview of all of Scripture, you describe God not just as a God of love, but as a God of *holy* love." Indeed, as we gain an overview of Romans, we come to the conclusion that an apt summary of Paul's teaching on the wrath of God would be that of Galatians 6:7: "A man reaps what he sows." Our choices have consequences.

Finally, we come to the question of why Paul begins his letter to the Romans in such a negative way. We wonder, *why does Paul begin his "good-news/bad-news" argument with the bad news*? And in truth it is not just the concept of *wrath* in chapter 1 that sounds so negative to our twentieth-century ears. It is in fact Paul's entire argument in chapters 1, 2, and the first half of 3 that many find disturbing. For what Paul sketches in for us in these three chapters is a very dark and depressing picture of human nature.

There is a question that has been volleyed back and forth in our society for many years. People of all religious and philosophical persuasions love to argue this question. The question is simply, "Do you think people are basically good or basically evil?" And this is no trivial question, for the way you answer it will have a direct bearing on your political beliefs, your educational beliefs, your economic beliefs, and your view of society. How, then, would Paul answer this question? As we read through the first three chapters of Romans, Paul leaves us no room for doubt. Quoting the psalmist, Paul declares in 3:10, "There is no one righteous, not even one."

Someone, after reading Romans 1, 2, and 3, once compared Paul to Dr. Norman Vincent Peale, the founder of *Guideposts* magazine and one of the leading Christian proponents of positive thinking. After comparing the two men, this person concluded, "Peale is appealing, but Paul is appalling!" And that's an understandable reaction to the opening pages of Romans: What a blow to our self-esteem! What a blow to our positive outlook on life and on ourselves! Why can't Paul begin by saying how good we are? Why doesn't Paul begin by helping us to feel better about ourselves?

At this point I want to be very clear about how the Bible views you and me, because there is an important place in our lives for the kind of positive attitude that is preached by Dr. Peale. The Bible teaches that we were originally created in the image of God, and God chose to purchase us with the blood of His Son Jesus because we are so precious in His eyes. We are people of value, and God has chosen to work out His eternal plan through our lives. Yet, without the righteousness of Christ, which comes through faith, all our wonderful potential as human beings must ultimately, tragically come to nothing. Sin has marred the image of God within us and has overshadowed all our attempts at righteousness. Only Jesus can restore God's image within us by covering us with *His* righteousness.

The exhilarating, exciting truth of Romans is that what at first glance appears to be bad news is in fact the best news imaginable: God has seen us at our worst—in all our sin and rebellion and deformity—and His message to us is still, "I love you." That's the power and wonder of the Christian gospel! Most of us go to church in our Sunday best, with our brightest smiles in place, our super-spiritual facades hiding our guilt, our tainted motives, our hurt, and our brokenness. But God sees through our facade and says, "I know all about you, and I still love you." And that's good news! That's much better news than if Paul had simply presented a false, rosy-tinted view of humanity that said, "God loves people because people are so good and wonderful."

God loves us amid all of our sin. As Paul writes in Romans 5:20, "Where sin increased, grace increased all the more." In a world that operates according to an impersonal moral order called "wrath," this message of love and forgiveness is God's intimately personal word to you and me.

A few years ago, Bruce Larson was the featured speaker at a Christian conference in the Midwest. There he met a woman who for years had been very active in ministering to the needs of hurting people in her church. But now it was she who was hurting. This woman had just been through radical surgery to remove cancerous tumors from her face. Nearly half the flesh of her face and one of her eyes had been removed, leaving her terribly deformed. She hid this deformity beneath a large white bandage that covered half her face.

During a break in the conference, this woman approached Larson and said, "I want to ask a favor of you."

"How can I help you?" he said.

"I know this sounds strange, but—well, I want to show you what I look like underneath this bandage."

He agreed to her request and the two of them went into another room where they could have some privacy. Then the woman removed the bandage, revealing the empty eye socket, the raw, unhealed scars around the patchwork skin grafts, and the gaping red areas where more reconstructive surgery was still needed. Then she put the bandage back on.

"Thank you, Bruce," she said. "I just wanted someone to see me as I really am, and to still love me."

That's Paul's message to us: God views us in all the deformity and ugliness of our sin. But God does not turn away from us. Rather, He reaches out to us, and the first words He shares with us are, "I love you."

And that's the best news we could ever hear.

Chapter 3

Creation Without, Conscience Within
(Romans 1:18–23)

Several years ago, I was at a conference center in the Colorado Rockies, speaking at a week-long conference sponsored by the Fellowship of Christian Athletes. Every morning, over a thousand young athletes met together while I presented a study from a Bible passage. Every evening we gathered in small groups for what FCAers call "buzz sessions." In these buzz sessions, the athletes had a chance to ask questions, offer opinions, or debate points I raised in my morning talk. The topics of these questions ranged from morality to dating to doctrine to the meaning of life.

During one buzz session, a young man said, "Ron, in your talk this morning you said our God is a God of love, that he unconditionally loves the whole world. Then you went on to say that Jesus Christ is the only way to God. You said Jesus is not just a better way, not just the best way, but the only way to God. But, Ron, what about the person who never hears about Jesus Christ? Is he saved or lost? And if he is lost because he never heard about Jesus, how can that be fair?"

This question is as old as the gospel itself. And it's a troubling question. What about those people in parts of Africa or Asia, the Indian subcontinent, the outlands of

Australia, the far-flung islands of the Pacific, all those remote places where the gospel has barely penetrated, or has not even begun to penetrate at all? What about the millions living in countries with Muslim governments which make it a capital crime to convert to another faith?

A friend of mine, a missionary who has committed himself to reaching the Muslim world for Jesus Christ, has traveled extensively in such countries as Lebanon, Egypt, Algeria, Libya, and Morocco. He says there is one thing that never ceases to amaze him in his travels. In remote villages, in the desert camps of Arab nomads, in all those places where people have never heard the Christian gospel, he hears Muslim people using words that sound like "tee-deh" and "koo-kah koo-lah." What they are talking about is Tide laundry detergent and Coca-Cola soft drinks. Arab villagers may be too poor to own an automatic washing machine, but they still buy a box of Tide and soak their clothes in the sudsy stuff before pounding them on a rock in the stream. They may be too poor to own a refrigerator, but they buy Coca-Cola and drink it luke-warm. Ironically, American industry has monopolized regions which the gospel has hardly begun to touch.

Hearing stories about such remote cultures, we have to wonder along with my young FCA friend, "What about the person who has never heard about Jesus Christ? How can it be fair for such a person to be lost in sin?" Yet, as we turn again to the first chapter of Romans, we find that these questions are in error. They are based on an assumption which Paul, writing under the inspiration of the Holy Spirit, refuses to make. Paul says to us, "Wrong. He had heard."

In Romans 1:18–23, Paul writes:

The wrath of God is being revealed from heaven against all the godlessness and wickedness of men who suppress the truth by their wickedness, since what may be known about God is plain to them, because God has made it plain to them. For since the creation of the world God's invisible qualities—his eternal power and divine nature—have been clearly seen, being understood from what has been made, so that men are without excuse. For although they knew God, they neither glorified him as God nor gave thanks to him, but their thinking became futile and their foolish hearts were darkened. Although they claimed to be wise, they became fools and exchanged the glory of the immortal God for images made to look like mortal men and birds and animals and reptiles.

The Bible teaches that God has revealed Himself to us in two ways, through two "books." One book is the book of special revelation, the Bible. God has revealed Himself to us by "breathing" His thoughts into His servants—people like Moses, David, Solomon, Matthew, Mark, Luke, John, and Paul—who then wrote those pages.

But God has also revealed Himself through the "book" of general revelation. The covers of this book are the day and the night. Its pages are the beauty of God's creation. Its print is the moral law of conscience that is inscribed upon the heart of every human being. Paul's thesis in Romans 1:18–23 is that God has revealed Himself to every person, either through the creation without or the conscience within. Therefore, the person who rejects God is without excuse.

Creation without. Conscience within. These are two inseparable components of God's "book" of general revelation to you and to me and to all of humanity.

Psalm 19 is one of many Scripture passages that affirm the revelation of God through the universe He has made: "The heavens declare the glory of God; the skies proclaim the work of His hands. Day after day they pour forth speech; night after night they display knowledge" (vv. 1–2). A similar passage is found in Psalm 8, in which the psalmist expresses to God his wonder when he considers "your heavens, the work of your fingers, the moon and the stars, which you have set in place" (v. 3). When those words were first written, people had a strong affinity with the earth, the skies, the seasons, the rhythms of the universe. As they looked at the great dome of the sky, as they watched the advancing seasons, as they witnessed the cycles and phases of life and death, they could clearly see the hand of an intelligent, personal Creator.

Today, even though most people have far less contact with nature than in the days of the psalmist, the heavens continue to declare the glory of God. For example, astronomer Robert Jastrow, in his book *God and the Astronomers*, describes the Big Bang theory as "the new story of Genesis."[1] Simply put, the Big Bang theory states that the universe began in a sudden explosion of light and energy. Many important features of this theory have already been convincingly proven. Jastrow explains, "The astronomical evidence leads to a biblical view of the origin of the world. The details differ, but the essential elements in the astronomical and biblical accounts of Genesis are the same: the chain of events leading to man commenced suddenly and sharply at a definite moment in time, in a flash of light and energy."[2]

The greatest and most insightful scientists of history—those like Galileo, Kepler, Newton, and Faraday—have always seen creation as the evidence of an intelligent Creator. It was Isaac Newton who observed, "This most beautiful system of the sun, planets and comets, could only proceed from the counsel and dominion of an intelligent and powerful Being." Similarly, Thomas Edison once wrote, "No one can study chemistry and see the wonderful way certain elements combine with the nicety of the most delicate machine ever invented and not conclude that there is a Great Engineer who is running this universe."

The late Dr. Wernher von Braun, who guided NASA's effort to land the first man on the moon, once said, "The public has a deep respect for the amazing scientific advances made within our lifetime. There is admiration for the scientific process of observation, or experimentation, of testing every concept to measure its validity. But it still bothers some people that we cannot prove scientifically that God exists. Must we light a candle to see the sun?" To put it another way, the existence of God is so evident in all He has made that to question this fact is to question our very senses. God has revealed Himself through the creation without.

God has also revealed Himself through the conscience within. Several years ago, Walter Matthau was being interviewed by reporters. He had just won an Academy Award and was riding a tide of tremendous fame, wealth, and success. He had the power to select any film project and name his price. One of the questions put to him by reporters was, "Mr. Matthau, in view of your enormous success and the honor of receiving an Oscar, would you describe yourself as 'happy' right now?"

Matthau was silent for a moment, and his expression deadpan. "Well, I guess I'm happy," he said slowly, "except I have this gnawing sense of guilt inside that somehow I'm doing something wrong." Walter Matthau was speaking for scores of people around the world who wrestle with a God who reveals Himself through the conscience within.

Anthropologists tell us there is a moral law of conscience that is essentially consistent from one culture to another. In books such as *The Abolition of Man* and *Mere Christianity*, C. S. Lewis concluded that this universal moral law is a powerful indicator of the existence of a single Author of morality and conscience.

> If anyone will take the trouble to compare the moral teaching of, say, the ancient Egyptians, Babylonians, Hindus, Chinese, Greeks and Romans, what will really strike him will be how very alike they are to each other and to our own . . . I need only to ask the reader to think what a totally different morality would mean. Think of a country where people were admired for running away in battle, or where a man felt proud of doublecrossing all the people who had been kindest to him. You might just as well try to imagine a country where two and two made five.[3]

The moral law of conscience operates in every man, in every woman, in every society, in every age. The conscience within testifies to the reality of God's eternal power and divine nature, so that we are all without excuse if we reject God.

Psalm 14:1 tells us, "The fool says in his heart, 'There is no God.' " I believe the reason the Bible describes an atheist as a "fool" is that only a fool would deny the truth that God Himself has revealed within us. Mahatma Gandhi, though not a Christian, nevertheless believed in God. He once remarked, "An atheist is a puzzle and a wonder. Here is an intelligent person who fights tenaciously against that which he firmly believes does not exist."

Such a man was the English philosopher and logician Bertrand Russell. One of the most brilliant, combative, and persistent atheists of this or any century, Russell was raised in the Puritan faith and later grew to reject that faith. After his death, Russell's daughter Katharine Tait wrote a book called *My Father Bertrand Russell* in which she observed, "Somewhere at the back of my father's mind, at the bottom of his heart, in the depths of his soul, there was an empty space that had once been filled by God and he never found anything else to put in it."[4]

How tragic! The denial of God is a denial of a truth that, deep down, refuses to be denied. An atheist literally has to lie to himself and reject the urging of his own heart. This is the human tragedy—and the human folly!—that Paul addresses in Romans 1. "For although they know God," he writes in verses 21 and 22, "they neither glorified him as God nor gave thanks to him, but their thinking became futile and their foolish hearts were darkened. Although they claimed to be wise, they became fools."

Through both special revelation (the Bible) and general revelation (the creation without and the conscience within), God draws men and women to a place of awareness of Himself, a place of conviction that

God is personally revealing Himself to them. In Romans 1, Paul describes those people who, having reached this place of awareness, choose to rebel. In so doing, as C. S. Lewis has sadly noted, "They are left to enjoy forever the terrible freedom they are given, and they are therefore enslaved." That "terrible freedom" is the most catastrophic fate any human soul can know.

But what about the person who comes to a place of awareness and conviction of God, and who wants to know more? This is when truly amazing things begin to happen. At this point, God will move the heavens and the earth to reveal the full light—Jesus, the Light of the World—to anyone who sincerely responds to the little light he has already received. This has been true throughout Scripture and throughout the history of the Christian church.

An example of this principle is found in Acts 8, the story of the Ethiopian eunuch. This African man, an important official in charge of the treasury of the queen of Ethiopia, was in the desert in Gaza, on the road between Jerusalem and the Ethiopian capital. He was sitting in his chariot, reading the book of Isaiah. As a result of special revelation (the Scripture he was reading) and general revelation (the creation without and the conscience within), this Ethiopian official had reached a point of awareness of God. Not only that, but he eagerly, hungrily desired to know more.

God responded to this man's sincere desire. He moved the heavens and the earth to reveal the full light of Jesus Christ to this man—and He did so in a way that defies logical explanation. God selected a man named Philip, who was in Samaria, about seventy miles north of Gaza. At the time, Philip was having an enormously effective preaching and healing ministry in Samaria, and vast numbers of people were turning their lives over to Jesus Christ. So successful was Philip's ministry that Acts 8:8 records that "there was great joy in that city." Suddenly, God told Philip to drop what he was doing and hurry south into the desert in Gaza. Such a command defies human logic, but fortunately for the spiritually hungry Ethiopian official, God's thoughts transcend and supercede human logic.

Philip obeyed and found the African man sitting in his chariot, reading this passage from Isaiah:

He was led like a sheep to the slaughter,
    and as a lamb before the shearer is silent,
    so he did not open his mouth.

Philip approached the man and asked if he understood what he was reading. "How can I," the man replied, "unless someone explains it to me?" So Philip sat down beside the African man and explained to him that the suffering Servant in Isaiah's prophecy, the One who had silently submitted to death for the sake of humankind, was Jesus the Messiah. It was Jesus who had fulfilled Isaiah's prophecy, who had come to redeem all people. The Ethiopian official, who had already received a little light, now experienced the full and complete light as Philip shared the gospel of Jesus Christ with him. He received Christ as Lord of his life and was baptized.

God reached out to the Ethiopian eunuch in Acts 8, just as He later reached out to a Gentile named Cornelius in Acts 10. Cornelius was a centurion, a high-ranking soldier in the Roman army. Though this man came from a completely pagan background and had never been taught about God, there was a glimmer of light within him. As a result of the creation without and the conscience within him, Cornelius had come to a place of awareness and conviction of God's reality, and he hungered to know more.

Once again, God moved the heavens and the earth to bring the full light of the gospel to someone who hungered after God. The means God chose in Cornelius's life was the apostle Peter. Of all people, Peter was the least likely to volunteer to minister to a non-Jew—and especially if that non-Jew was a soldier in the hated Roman army! But God came to Peter in a dream and said, in effect, "Peter, the gospel must go out to all people, not just the Jews. You've got to break down your prejudice toward Gentile people. As a first step, I'm sending you to a Roman named Cornelius."

Peter went to Cornelius and added the full light of the gospel to the little light Cornelius already had. As a result, not only Cornelius but many of his friends and relatives also yielded their lives to Jesus Christ that day.

Paul himself saw God perform such miracles not once, but many times. On their first missionary journey, Paul and Barnabas went to Cypress, where they found people sincerely responding to the light they already had. So God, through Paul and Barnabas, gave them the full light of the gospel. From Cypress, Paul and Barnabas went to Asia Minor, where they encountered hardship, persecution, and—yes!—spiritually hungry people who desired the full light of the gospel. Later Paul went to Europe, where he met a prominent businesswoman named Lydia. Acts 16:14 says that Lydia already was aware of God, that she worshiped God, but she had never heard the good news of Jesus Christ, so "the Lord opened her heart to respond to Paul's message."

And that has been the pattern throughout Christian history: God reveals Himself to every person through the creation without, the conscience within. As men and women sincerely respond to that spark of revelation within them, God will move the heavens and the earth to bring them into the bright day of His saving light. As James 4:8 puts it, "Come near to God and He will come near to you."

Clearly, the question we must ask ourselves is not, What about those people in Africa, Asia, or India who never heard about Jesus? Rather, the pivotal question that confronts you and me is, What about all those people both in remote parts of the world and right on my own block and at my job and in my family who are coming to a place of awareness and conviction about God? Am I willing, like Philip, like Peter, like Paul and Barnabas, to be used by God to give those people the full light of the gospel? Am I willing to share the gospel with those in my own sphere of influence? Am I willing to be involved in prayerfully and financially supporting world missionary efforts? Am I willing to be God's channel for ministry as He moves the heavens and the earth to reveal His Son Jesus to those who sincerely seek Him?

In his book *Love, Acceptance and Forgiveness*, Jerry Cook tells the story of a young unmarried couple living together in a "free love" commune. He was a drug pusher, and she was a drug user. One day, as they were using drugs together, he said to her, "I wish I could quit using this stuff."

"You want to be free of drugs?" the young woman said. "If you trusted in Jesus Christ as your Savior, He would deliver you."

"Huh?" he said, surprised. "What do you mean, 'trust in Jesus Christ as my Savior.' How do I do that?"

She hesitated. "Never mind," she said, "I'm not going to tell you."

"Why not?"

"Because if you become a Christian, you'll leave this commune and I'll never see you again."

He kept after her to explain the gospel to him, and finally she gave in and explained the plan of salvation. "If all this is true," he said finally, "why are you in this place, doing drugs with a guy like me? Why aren't you going to church and living like a Christian?"

"I was raised in a Christian home," the young woman replied. "But I decided a few years ago that I just wanted to live my life my own way."

A few moments later, the young man prayed and yielded his life to Christ. He was delivered from his addiction to drugs and—just as his girlfriend feared—he left the commune and never returned. He had begun his spiritual journey with only a faint flicker of spiritual awareness, and had been led to the Lord by a self-willed, rebellious non-Christian. As Jerry Cook observed, "The gospel is so simple that even a non-Christian can lead another person to Christ . . . . The power is in the gospel, not in the presentation."[5]

The young woman continued in the self-destructive lifestyle she had chosen, enjoying the "terrible freedom" of a life without Jesus Christ. Tragically, although she knew God, she neither glorified nor thanked Him. She had received so much light during the years she lived in a Christian home, yet she willfully allowed her foolish heart to be darkened.

You and I have received such a rich supply of the light of God's revelation. All around us are people with just a little light—yet they desire to know more. They are coming to an awareness of the God you and I already know so well. The Holy Spirit is probably bringing someone to your mind even as you read these words. He is nudging you to go and share the Light of the World with that friend, that relative, that co-worker He has brought to your mind.

You and I have been given the gift of God's special revelation in the Bible and His general revelation in the creation without and the conscience within. Now the question that confronts us is: What will we do with the light we have received?

Chapter 4

The Worst Sins
(Romans 1:24–32)

A number of years ago, I was appointed to a denominational task force in the Midwest to consider this issue: Should an avowed, practicing homosexual be ordained to the pastoral ministry? During our discussions, it became clear that our task force divided into two positions, representing two distinct wings of the denomination. On one side were those who took a theologically liberal viewpoint, saying, "Yes, in certain circumstances a practicing homosexual can be ordained as a pastor in our denomination."

I firmly opposed that position then as I do today, because I believe we cannot ordain a person who is unrepentant with regard to the sin of homosexuality, any more than we should ordain an unrepentant thief, an unrepentant gossip, or any other person who would profess rather than repent of his sin. God demands a lifestyle of repentance, integrity, and obedience from those who shepherd the congregations of His Church.

So when my turn came to speak, I said, "The real issue of our debate here is not the issue of homosexuality. The real issue is the authority of Scripture. The question is not so much, What do we do with the homosexual? The question is, What do we do with the Word of God? The Bible takes a clear position against homosexual behavior.

I don't see how this task force can take any position that conflicts with the clear position of God's Word. To me the answer is plain: No, we cannot ordain a practicing homosexual to the pastoral ministry and still maintain our biblical integrity."

One of the passages I cited for scriptural support was Romans 1, where Paul—in his toughest, most prosecutorial style—states that the wrath of God is being revealed against all forms of wickedness, including the sin of unrepentant homosexual practice:

> Therefore God gave them over in the sinful desires of their hearts to sexual impurity for the degrading of their bodies with one another. They exchanged the truth of God for a lie, and worshiped and served created things rather than the Creator— who is forever praised. Amen.

> Because of this, God gave them over to shameful lusts. Even their women exchanged natural relations for unnatural ones. In the same way the men also abandoned natural relations with women and were inflamed with lust for one another. Men committed indecent acts with other men, and received in themselves the due penalty for their perversion (Romans 1:24–27).

Paul's words are so unambiguously clear on the subject of homosexual practice that you might wonder what is left to debate. Yet from that point on, the debate not only continued, it intensified. And as the discussion heated up, I saw another extreme position emerge, a position that to my mind is every bit as misguided as that of the theological liberals. Each week, as our task force met together, we would find on our table a ream of letters from evangelical, Bible-believing Christians.

Written in the language of hate, these letters used some of the most demeaning terms imaginable to describe homosexual people.

Reading these bitter, vindictive letters, I began to wonder if our task force wasn't debating the wrong question. Maybe we shouldn't be asking if we should ordain practicing homosexuals to the ministry. Instead, perhaps we should be asking: Can we fail to unconditionally love homosexual people and still maintain our biblical integrity? For me, the answer was clearly, No! We must unconditionally love even those who are unlovely because of their sin. If we fail to love as Jesus loved, then we have betrayed everything we stand for as followers of Christ.

There are very few issues that more aptly symbolize the brokenness of the world we live in than the issue of homosexuality. And in this age of permissiveness, pornography, and the AIDS epidemic, it is critically important that we understand what the Word of God does and does not say in its treatment of homosexuality. In Romans 1, Paul writes very clearly about a form of behavior, not a class of people. He doesn't condemn people who have homosexual tendencies. He talks specifically about those men and women who choose, in their God-given free will, to exchange a normal heterosexual marriage relationship for homosexual relationships—men committing indecent acts with men, and women with women.

There are other men and women—including many Christians—who struggle with homosexual *tendencies* and with homosexual *temptation*. In much the same way that heterosexuals wrestle against sexual temptation, many homosexually-oriented people experience an internal conflict between the desire to live a chaste life versus the temptation to sexual sin. They carry the burden of spiritual, emotional, and psychological dynamics that are far too complex to adequately deal with here.

Having counseled scores of homosexually-oriented people, I know they struggle not only against temptation, but against the bitter memories of a painful past. Almost invariably, they are dealing not only with their own tendency to sin, but with the memories of having been sinned against in the past. They have been humiliated, perhaps even violated, and often their hurts go back to childhood. Those who struggle with homosexual tendencies deserve our compassion, support, and empathy, not our scorn.

Estimates vary, but it is likely that there are around 15 million people in America who are either homosexual or bi-sexual in their orientation. One of these is a friend of mine named Kevin, who I came to know when I lived in the Midwest. Kevin lived in the downtown area of a major city, an area known as a hub of homosexual activity. Around the time I came to know him, Kevin yielded his life to Jesus Christ. As a new Christian, he read the Bible daily, and his study of Scripture convinced him that homosexual practice is a sin.

Kevin became involved with a Bible study group, and within a few weeks he trusted the group enough to reveal to them the kind of life he had been living. He told his Christian friends he had decided to leave his homosexual lifestyle, and he asked them to pray for him, to hold him accountable for his actions, and to check on his progress. His friends loved him enough to do as he asked. They also encouraged him to seek the help of a Christian psychologist. With the counsel and encouragement of his friends and the psychologist, Kevin experienced healing in his sexual identity. Today he is married and has a family, and is completely happy serving God in his new life.

The reason I tell you the story of my friend Kevin is not to suggest that this happily-ever-after ending is the norm when sexually confused people seek to change. Tragically, Kevin's story is an extremely rare occurrence. Over the years, I've seen scores of people who have made a public profession of Christ, and who have sincerely felt they had experienced healing in their sexual identity as a result of their conversion. Yet I would have to confess that out of all these cases, probably 90 to 95 percent went back to a homosexual lifestyle within six months. We have to ask ourselves, "Why?"

There are too many reasons to number here. But I want to suggest just one reason that I firmly believe to be a real part of the problem: our failure as Christians to build communities where homosexually-oriented people can be held accountable within an atmosphere of unconditional love, acceptance, and forgiveness. Until our churches become authentic healing communities, we will continue to see a tragically high failure rate among those who seek healing in their sexual identities.

To bring these issues into better focus, consider the following three questions: First, how many Bible-believing Christians do you suppose have marched, protested, carried signs, and chanted slogans against the homosexual community in the past ten years? Second, how many Bible-believing Christians do you suppose have volunteered to give their time to the AIDS ward of a hospital, bringing a ministry of compassion to homosexual AIDS victims? Third, which of the above responses would God most likely honor as a means of bringing people to Christ? Which would be a more effective way of penetrating this broken world with the good news of Jesus Christ—protest or compassion?

Perhaps the most important principle you and I should learn from this passage in Romans is that Christians are to be *pro*-active in this world, not merely *re*-active. We are to be *pro-Christ* before we are anti-anything.

As I have traveled throughout this country and abroad, I have become aware of many churches that have become known for the things they oppose. I've seen churches that are militantly anti-pornography, anti-homosexual, or anti-secular humanism. I'm convinced that one of the great Satanic strategies of our age is to seduce us into becoming so anti-something that we lose sight of the fact that first, foremost, and above all else, we are called to be pro-Jesus Christ. Everything we do as we seek to make a positive difference in this broken world must be focused on one goal, the goal of lifting up Jesus Christ.

That was the goal of my friend Gary. A talented Christian musician, composer, and arranger, Gary was suffering from a cough and cold while producing a city-wide holiday program. Two weeks after the program, Gary called and asked for prayer. He thought his cold was going into pneumonia, and he was checking into the hospital. When the test results came in, the doctors concluded that Gary did indeed have pneumonia—a complication arising from AIDS. Visiting Gary at his hospital bedside, he told me about the diagnosis, and that he had come out of a homosexual lifestyle a couple years earlier. He had rededicated his life to Christ and was now married.

Months passed, and Gary underwent treatment in the AIDS ward of a large hospital. The next time I saw him, he had lost a lot of weight. It was clear that the disease was swiftly ravaging his body. He told me about his experience in the AIDS ward, living among scores of dying young men—many of whom were skeletal foreshadows of Gary's own fate. Gary went from man to man, sharing with each one his unshakable faith in Jesus Christ. A number of the young men Gary witnessed to yielded their lives to Christ in the last days of their lives.

"Jesus went to the lepers," Gary told me. "It seems to me that people with AIDS are the lepers of our day. If Jesus were here today, He'd go to the AIDS ward. What saddens me is that I didn't see any Christians reaching out with compassion to those people who were dying of AIDS." He told me about many of his Christian friends who began to pull away from him when they discovered he had AIDS. They stopped visiting, they stopped phoning, they left him alone. I remember the grateful look in Gary's eyes when I would do something as small as holding his hand while praying with him, or hugging him when I said good-bye. "Except for my wife and my family," he said, "you're the only one who will do that."

Over the next weeks, Gary lost eighty pounds as the virus continued to attack his nervous system. His sight failed. He lost control of his body functions. Every breath became a life-and-death struggle. His pain was continuous. The critical care nurse working on his case told me, "This is the worst case of physical suffering

I've witnessed in twenty-one years of nursing." A few weeks later, at the age of thirty-two, Gary died.

I have often thought of my friend Gary as a symbol of how we in the church have responded to people who wrestle with the hurt and the temptation of their homosexual tendencies. All too often, the church says to these people, *"You change*—then we'll love you," rather than, "We love you right now, despite the awfulness of your self-destructive sin. And we're going to love you enough to hold you accountable. We're going to love you with tough love so God can bring healing in this area of your life. But whether you stumble again or whether you find total victory over this sin, we are still going to love you, because the gospel demands nothing less than that."

Several years ago, a pastor received a letter. The writer of the letter asked the pastor to read it to the congregation. This is what it said:

Dear friends:

I've been a part of this church for years, and have come to know some of you very well. However, there is something about me that none of you know: I am a homosexual. I wish I could tell you who I am, but I can't believe you would still love me if I did. You all talk about the love of Jesus, yet I've seen a lot of hatred among you—hatred not only for sin, but for the sinner. I've heard the jokes you tell about people like me, and the words you use to describe people with my problems. It's ugly, and it frightens me.

I'm not proud of my past. I pray that God will take away these desires. I'm praying for strength to resist temptation. But I feel all alone in my struggle.

If I confessed my sin and my struggle to you right now, would it change our relationship? Would you continue to accept me as a child of God? Would you continue to pray for me? Could you still love me? I desperately need your help, your prayers, and your friendship right now, but I'm afraid to reveal myself to you. I just can't take that chance.

> Yours in Christ,
> A sinner

I've spent many hours listening to the painful, lonely stories of Christians struggling with homosexuality. I've also seen the kind of stereotyping, the ridiculing, the off-color jokes that so many in the evangelical community direct at the homosexual community. And I have to believe that we would do better to make fewer jokes about homosexuals, while offering more prayers for them. Would Jesus really have us simply write off the 15 million people in this country who are confused in their sexual orientation? If we are to fulfill Christ's Great Commandment to love and His Great Commission to be His witnesses, we *cannot* write off any individual, regardless of his sin.

Paul, in Romans 1, condemns the sin of homosexual practice, in no uncertain terms. And so must you and I. But do you know what is the *really* disturbing aspect of Romans 1 for you and me? It's the fact that Paul doesn't stop there. We could feel so comfortable if only Paul would talk about the sin of homosexuality and leave it

at that. But he *doesn't* leave it at that! He continues,
verses 28 to 32:

Furthermore, since they did not think it
worthwhile to retain the knowledge of God, he
gave them over to a depraved mind, to do what
ought not to be done. They have become filled with
every kind of wickedness, evil, greed and depravity.
They are full of envy, murder, strife, deceit and
malice. They are gossips, slanderers, God-haters,
insolent, arrogant and boastful; they invent ways of
doing evil; they disobey their parents; they are
senseless, faithless, heartless, ruthless. Although
they know God's righteous decree that those who
do such things deserve death, they not only
continue to do these very things but also approve of
those who practice them.

Now Paul has really done it, hasn't he? He's begun
talking about the wrong people! He's talking about you
and me! Here Paul has arrived at the lowest rungs of the
most brilliant argument ever made about the nature of
man—and what does he talk about? Your sins and
mine! Sins of pride and self-righteousness, sins of gossip
and slander, sins of jealousy and envy! In our shame, we
have found ourselves on Paul's list right alongside those
who commit homosexual acts.

If we're honest, we really enjoy pointing the finger of
blame and putting the other fellow in the wrong, because
that makes us feel good about ourselves by contrast. The
person who willfully chooses the homosexual lifestyle
provides us with an example against which we can
smugly compare ourselves. But Paul won't let us off the
hook that easily. Inspired by the Holy Spirit, he
punctures our pride and convicts our hearts of sin.

That is also the message of C. S. Lewis, who makes it clear in *Mere Christianity* that sexual sins are not, as some believe, the worst sins. He writes:

> The sins of the flesh are bad but they are the least bad of all sins. All the worst pleasures are purely spiritual: the pleasure of putting other people in the wrong, of bossing and patronizing and spoiling sport, and backbiting; the pleasures of power, of hatred . . . . That is why a cold, self-righteous prig who goes regularly to church may be far nearer to hell than a prostitute.

Strong words, shocking words—and Lewis hastens to add, "But, of course, it is better to be neither."[1]

It has been said that the ground is level at the foot of the cross. We have no reason to feel superior to any other person, regardless of that person's sin. We are all sinful. We are all broken. Our relationships are distorted—if not by sexual sin, then by sins of hypocrisy, pride, an unbridled tongue, envy, strife, or greed. We have no righteousness to claim but the righteousness of Jesus Christ.

Before Fiorello LaGuardia was elected mayor of New York in 1933, he was a judge in the municipal court. One bitterly cold day, a trembling, rag-clad man was brought before Judge LaGuardia's bench, charged with stealing a loaf of bread. Looking to the rear of the courtroom, LaGuardia saw the man's wife and children huddled together. The children were crying. Peering down at the man, LaGuardia said, "What do you have to say for yourself?"

The man looked down at the floor and shook his head. "It's true," he mumbled. "I stole the bread. I've been out of work, and my family was starving. But what I did was wrong."

"Yes," said LaGuardia. "What you did was wrong, and the law makes no exception. I find you guilty and sentence you to a ten-dollar fine." He rapped his gavel, then reached behind him and took his felt hat off the hat-tree. Handing the hat to the bailiff, he dug into his pants pocket and pulled out a ten-dollar bill, and tossed it into the hat. "We're going to do things a little differently than usual," LaGuardia said to the astonished man. "Just this once, the court is going to pay the fine to the accused. Furthermore, I'm going to fine everybody in this courtroom fifty cents for living in a town where a man has to steal bread in order to feed his family. Mr. Bailiff, collect the fines in that hat and give them to this defendant! Oh, and see that the hat comes back to me."

The hat was duly passed, and the man—hardly able to believe the reality of the grace he had received—left the courtroom with his joyful family and a total of $47.50 to stake him to a new future.

That's the kind of overflowing, unmerited grace you and I have received amid our own sinfulness and wretchedness. And it is our obligation—and ultimately it is our *joy*—to show that kind of overflowing love, acceptance, and forgiveness to those around us who have stumbled and fallen. When these qualities become evident in our lives, then our churches will no longer be places where sexually confused people are condemned. Rather, our churches will become communities where *all* people, no matter what their sin, find healing and forgiveness.

Chapter 5

A Passion for Splinters
(Romans 2:1–3:20)

The year was 1964. A well-known writer was the guest on a popular radio talk-show in New York City. The discussion turned to the troubled decade of the 1930s, and the writer began to detail the failures of the President who oversaw the worst years of the Depression, Herbert Hoover.

The writer criticized what he saw as Hoover's insensitivity in failing to provide work for the unemployed. He excoriated Hoover for ordering the Army to clamp down on protesting veterans in 1932. He not only disparaged Hoover's actions, but his character.

As he talked, the talk-show host scribbled a note and passed it across the studio table. The writer paused in mid-sentence and glanced at the note. It read simply: "Did you know he's listening to you?"

It was true. The former President was on his deathbed in a New York City hotel suite. Plagued with insomnia in his later years, Hoover regularly tuned in the show for companionship in the long sleepless nights. "That was a shock," the writer later recalled. "I had been thinking of him as a symbol for so long that it had never occurred to me that he was still a living, hurting old man."[1]

So it is with you and me. The people we talk about, ridicule, criticize, and judge, whether they are in the news or even in our own churches, easily become mere symbols to us. What gets lost behind the caricatures we construct of one another is the palpable reality of a living human soul.

In Romans 2, the apostle Paul confronts our judgmental pride, yanking our threadbare self-righteousness from under our feet. "You, therefore, have no excuse," Paul tells us in Romans 2:1, "you who pass judgment on someone else, for at whatever point you judge the other, you are condemning yourself, because you who pass judgment do the same things." With the relentless eloquence of a criminal prosecutor, Paul strips away our right to feel superior and judgmental toward "those sinners over there." He backs us into a corner and wrings from us the reluctant confession that we have no righteousness of our own—only the righteousness of Jesus that covers the wretchedness of our sin.

Clearly, the Scriptures leave us no room to judge, to gossip, to feel self-righteous. Why, then, have the very sins that Paul condemns in Romans 2 infected the body of Christ like a deadly virus? Why is the landscape of Christendom littered with the battered and wounded souls of those *we* have judged, mistreated, and slandered?

In *The Weight of Glory*, C. S. Lewis confronts the tragedy of our sin by pointing us to the awesome burden each of us is called to shoulder in Christian humility—the burden of our neighbor's eternal soul. As Lewis observes, it's a burden too heavy for proud, self-righteous, judgmental people to bear. He writes:

It may be possible for each of us to think too much of his own potential glory hereafter; it is hardly possible for him to think too often or too deeply about that of his neighbor. The load, or weight, or burden of my neighbor's glory should be laid daily on my back, a load so heavy that only humility can carry it, and the backs of the proud will be broken. It is a serious thing . . . to remember that the dullest and most uninteresting person you talk to may one day be a creature which, if you saw it now, you would be strongly tempted to worship, or else a horror and a corruption such as you now meet, if at all, only in a nightmare. All day long we are, in some degree, helping each other to one or the other of these destinations . . . .

There are no ordinary people. You have never talked to a mere mortal. Nations, cultures, arts, civilization—these are mortal, and their life is to ours as the life of a gnat. But it is immortals whom we joke with, work with, marry, snub, and exploit—immortal horrors or everlasting splendors . . . .

Our charity must be a real and costly love, with deep feeling for the sins in spite of which we love the sinner.[2]

A few years ago, the body of a young woman was pulled from the harbor waters of New York City. She had jumped from a bridge, taking her own life. Her body was laid out upon the dock and inspected for clues to the reason for her suicide. In the pocket of her coat, a piece of paper was found. There were only two words written upon it, as if she had started to scrawl a last despairing message, but was unable to continue. It read, "They said—" A living, hurting young woman had been treated as a *thing* to be judged and ridiculed, and she could no longer endure being the object of rumors and misunderstanding. What a concise and eloquent expression of a human soul, tormented by the unfeeling judgments of others: "They said—"

In James 4:11–12 we find a parallel passage to that of Romans 2: "Brothers, do not slander one another . . . . There is only one Lawgiver and Judge, the one who is able to save and destroy. But you—who are you to judge your neighbor?" I think most of us, when reading such a passage, tend to think, "Well, I haven't slandered anyone. I haven't judged anyone."

But the Greek word rendered "slander" in this passage comes from two Greek words meaning "talk down." And who among us has not at some time "talked down" the reputation, the character of some other person? We're very subtle and creative about it, often fooling even ourselves. We don't say anything overtly negative at all. We mask our intentions so carefully.

Often we start with a disclaimer. "I really don't mean to be critical, but—" Or, "Perhaps I shouldn't say this about him, but—" Or, slyest of all, "I only mention this so you can be praying, but—" And we go on to say something that demeans another person's character or reputation.

There are few sins that the Bible condemns so unsparingly—and few sins that are so common and fascinating to us all—as the sins of gossip. But in these passages, Paul and James not only admonish us not to speak critically of others; they warn us not to *judge* one another. That is, God, speaking to us through His servants Paul and James, calls us to a process of learning to release other people from our judgment. Why? Because, to judge someone rightly, we would have to know all there is to know about that person. To discern the state of another person's character, we would actually need to *be God.* I think it's safe to say that you and I are not God. You and I do not know what lies beneath the surface of another person's heart.

What Paul tells us in Romans 2 and what James tells us in James 4 are simply echoes of the words of our Lord Himself in Matthew 7:1–5:

> Do not judge, or you too will be judged. For in the same way you judge others, you will be judged, and with the measure you use, it will be measured to you.

> Why do you look at the speck of sawdust in your brother's eye and pay no attention to the plank in your own eye? How can you say to your brother, 'Let me take the speck out of your eye,' when all the time there is a plank in your own eye? You hypocrite, first take the plank out of your own eye, and then you will see clearly to remove the speck from your brother's eye.

Jesus confronts us with the fact that, in our heart of hearts, we really *enjoy* hunting for splinters—especially when the splinter is in someone else's eye. Let's admit it: Most of us have an absolute *passion* for splinters. And it's amazing, isn't it, that we can find our neighbor's splinter with that oversized log in our own eye.

Jesus, Paul, and James agree on this: Our job as Christians is to build one another up in a spirit of encouragement, affirmation, and forgiveness, not to tear each other down with criticism and malicious gossip.

This doesn't mean we are never to be discerning, that we are never to reach out and lovingly confront someone when we see an area of weakness or sin in his or her life. Galatians 6:1 makes it clear that there will be times when we must confront one another, gently and humbly. Nor does it mean that there is never a place for church discipline; Matthew 18 and 1 Corinthians 5 tell us that Christians are accountable to the church for their actions and their lifestyle.

But the purpose of confronting sin—whether individually or through a disciplinary process—is not punishment but the restoration of the sinner. There is nothing restoring about judging others or about spreading rumors.

Those who fall into serious error are *wounded* people. They need to be surrounded by people of grace, forgiveness, and understanding. The world is trying to tear them down; the church must be a sanctuary where they can be built up again. For every critic they have in the world, they're going to need ten or twenty brothers and sisters saying, "I believe in you, I know you can make it, I'm praying for you. If you fall, I'll be here to lift you up again."

When I was in school, doing graduate studies, we had chapel services twice a week. At one of these services, we had a guest speaker who had flown in to speak to us. His talk was not one of the more memorable chapel sermons I had heard. In fact, I found it boring, disjointed, and hard to follow. I didn't get a thing out of it.

After chapel, I met one of my classmates in the hall. "What a waste of time," I said. "He sure didn't have much to say, did he?"

My friend looked at me with an uncomfortable expression. "Ron," he said, "I don't think you know all the facts. I just heard that he got a call from home a couple of hours before he was to speak. It was his wife calling with news that their son had been killed in a traffic accident. Whatever you think of his talk, he decided to go out there and give that talk first before flying back home to comfort his wife and bury his son."

Those words continue to haunt me: "Ron, I don't think you know all the facts." That's always the way it is whenever we choose to pass along our judgment, our criticism, our juicy bit of gossip about some other person: We don't know all the facts. The people we judge and snub are not symbols; they are immortal human souls, wounded and hurting and needy. When at last we have removed the logs from our own eyes—the logs of arrogance, of pride, of self-righteousness, of hypocrisy—then our passion for the splinters of others will be replaced by a genuine *compassion* for wounded human souls.

Chapter 6

And Now,
the Good News
(Romans 3:21–4:25)

Karen's life had never been easy. She had endured the tyranny of an abusive stepfather since early childhood, chose the life of a teenage runaway at age fifteen, lived with an abusive boyfriend at sixteen, was pregnant and abandoned at seventeen. At age nineteen, some Christian friends reached out to her, befriended her, and helped her come to a place of faith in Jesus as Lord of her life. Then tragedy struck when her beloved three-year-old boy was diagnosed with leukemia.

"God will heal your little boy," some of her Christian friends told her, "if you have enough faith."

Enough faith? She wondered how much faith was "enough." For the next six months she poured out her love for her little boy in prayers for his healing. She desperately fought her doubts while her son's condition worsened, and as he went through a series of painful treatments. For a while, his disease went into remission and Karen's hopes brightened. But in the end he died. Karen was devastated.

Tormented by guilt and doubt, she accused herself of causing her son's death. "It's *my* fault," she reasoned. "If I had only had more faith, God would have healed my little boy."

It wasn't long before the accusations she directed against herself began to poison her relationship with God. What kind of monstrous God would let a little boy suffer and die like that? How dare God stamp her prayers "Insufficient Faith" and return them unanswered? If all her tearful, desperate prayers for her little boy were not enough, then what was?

Karen left the church and her Christian friends, saying, "The God you believe in is either a monster or a myth. I'll never believe in such a God again!"

Soon afterward, she became involved with another abusive man, by whom she had a second child, a daughter. During a fit of drunken rage, he beat Karen severely. After he went to sleep, she crept out of the house with her infant daughter. She was defeated and afraid, alone and penniless, a twenty-two-year-old single mother without any education or skills to make her way in the world.

That night, Karen went to a Christian women's shelter. Determined to have nothing to do with God, she accepted food and care for herself and her baby girl but spurned the shelter's message of hope. "I don't want to hear about your God," she told the director of the shelter, Mrs. Oliver. "He's already let me down too many times. My prayers weren't enough to save my little boy from dying. I won't let God disappoint me like that again."

"I don't pretend to know how it feels to lose a little boy," said Mrs. Oliver. "But I know how it feels to pray for a loved one to be healed, and to have God answer 'No' to those prayers. When Burt, my husband, died of cancer last year, he was forty-five years old. I prayed for him to get better, but he never did. God allowed Burt to die not because I lacked faith, but because God wanted Burt home with Him. To me, faith isn't a magic spell we put on God to get Him to do our bidding. Faith is just trusting that God loves us and helps us get through the worst that life can throw at us."

It was a long time before Karen was able to accept that. But people from the shelter and a nearby church continued to care for Karen, accepting her doubts and anger while loving her unconditionally. Gradually, Karen's heart began to soften. Two weeks after her arrival, she left the shelter with the prospect of a new job and an apartment with a Christian roommate. More important, she left with a newly revived faith, rooted in a realistic trust in the faithfulness of God.

Here in the third chapter of Romans, Paul begins his masterful treatise on the subject of faith. As we have already seen, the theme of the first section of Romans has been *sin*. But with the first two words of Romans 3:21, Paul gives us a transition from sin to salvation, from bad news to good news, from despair to faith. The two little words that kick off the "good news" section of Romans are: "But now . . . ." It's as if Paul, the relentless prosecutor, suddenly pauses, takes a deep breath, and switches sides. Now Paul takes up our defense. In Romans 3:21–28, he gives us the *solution* to our human crisis as he writes:

> But now a righteousness from God, apart from law, has been made known, to which the Law and the Prophets testify. This righteousness from God comes through faith in Jesus Christ to all who believe. There is no difference, for all have sinned and fall short of the glory of God, and are justified freely by His grace through the redemption that

came by Christ Jesus. God presented him as a sacrifice of atonement through faith in His blood. He did this to demonstrate his justice, because in his forbearance he had left the sins committed beforehand unpunished—he did it to demonstrate his justice at the present time, so as to be just and the one who justifies those who have faith in Jesus.

Where, then, is boasting? It is excluded. On what principle? On that of observing the law? No, but on that of faith. For we maintain that a man is justified by faith apart from observing the law.

In this passage, Paul confronts a major error that has crept into twentieth-century Christianity: the idea that "faith" is something we accomplish in our own strength. Paul makes it emphatically clear in these verses that authentic biblical faith is God's attribute, not ours. The focus of faith is *God's* grace, *God's* power—not our effort.

Faith is not a quantifiable "thing" we summon from within ourselves. There is no such thing as having "enough" faith or "not enough" faith. Biblical faith is simple trust in the infinite faithfulness and power of God. That's why Jesus said that faith the size of a mustard seed can move mountains. Jesus wanted to make it abundantly clear that the focus of the mountain-moving power is on the One who *made* the mountain, not the limited human being with his or her tiny particle of faith.

Those well-intentioned Christians who told Karen God would heal her little boy *"if* you have enough faith" did an enormous disservice to *her.* They placed the burden for her child's healing on her. So when her child died, she had the added burden of guilt to deal with, along with her grief. Moreover, if her son had gotten well, she would have been able to boast that her own faith was responsible. Yet Paul says, "Where, then, is boasting? It is excluded." Why? Because the very focus of faith is God, not us. It is God who justifies us, God who redeems us, God who heals us, God who is faithful. Our part is simply to trust the faithfulness of God to us.

Over and over, I see the guilt and frustration people heap upon themselves as they struggle to become people of "great faith." But I'm convinced God never intended you and me to have "great faith" as the goal of our lives. We are rather to be ordinary men and women who simply place our trust in the *great faithfulness* of God. Once we have grasped this concept, then our striving after "enough" faith is over. We can rest in the fact that we already have "enough" faith.

When a Christian goes through the deep waters of testing, when a child is seriously ill, when a business is failing, when a marriage is crumbling, the message of Romans is not, "If you just have enough faith, everything will come out all right," but, "God is faithful and will never forsake you, no matter what you are going through." When it is God's faithfulness rather than our own faith that is our focus, then there is no room for the "ego trip" of becoming a person of great faith. Nor is there room for the "guilt trip" of insufficient faith. The results of our prayers rest with God, not with us.

E. Stanley Jones, the nineteenth-century missionary to India, learned this truth the hard way. After years of intense, workaholic effort among the Indian people, accompanied by uncounted hours on his knees in prayer, Jones finally came to a point of exhaustion and spiritual collapse. In despair, he went to his knees and cried out, "Lord, I can strive no more for you! Come, live your life through me!" That moment was a great breakthrough, the beginning of a revolutionary phase in the life of E. Stanley Jones. Though he continued to work hard and pray fervently, his heart was changed. His work was transformed from a crushing burden to a labor of love, carried out with renewed freedom and vitality. Jones was finally able to trust God's faithfulness, not his own efforts, to achieve the fruit of his ministry in India.

Notice that when Paul uses the word *faith* in Romans, he points us back to the Old Testament. In Romans 1:17, Paul quotes Habakkuk 2:4, "The righteous will live by his faith." The New International Version of Habakkuk 2:4 adds a footnote that reads, "Or *faithfulness*." The original Hebrew understanding of the word *faith* did not merely connote "belief." The Hebrews understood *faith* to mean the faithfulness of God, and that's the understanding Paul points us to in Romans. He wants us to understand that faith is an attribute not of human beings, but of God.

Understand, too, that the Hebrew word for *faith* (*'emunah*) Paul cites in Habakkuk 2:4 is rich in synonyms and subtle shadings. It conveys not only faithfulness, but fidelity, stability, security, and—most importantly—truth. It's the word from which we get that resounding affirmative *Amen*. It's a word that connotes rock-solid, objective truth. For, in fact, that is what the Christian faith is all about: *truth*.

We do not trust in a fantasy. We trust the God of objective reality. This is where the Christian faith distinguishes itself from so many cults, crazes, and philosophies of our age. In this supposedly scientifically-minded era of the late twentieth century, our culture has gone on a binge of irrationality and subjective fantasy. A common catch-phrase of this decade is, "You have your truth, and I have my truth," as if it doesn't even matter what the *true* truth is!

Many Christians seek to evangelize their non-Christian friends by saying, "Come to Christ because he *works*. He worked for me, and he'll work for you." How is this statement any different from the affirmation of those in the cults or in the New Age movement or in some motivational seminar saying, "Try my belief system! It works! Experience peace of mind! Find wealth! Attain purpose in life! Discover healing in your marriage! This thing really works!" The problem with such claims is that a lot of things "work," at least for a while. Zen and TM can help you experience tranquility. Drugs can induce euphoria. The acquisition of wealth induces a false sense of security and power. These things "work," but are they reliable, dependable, faithful? Are they *true*?

Certainly, as we share our faith with others, we want to bear witness to what God has accomplished in our lives. We want to tell others how God has healed our broken marriage, or given us greater peace of mind, or filled our lives with meaning—but we ought to be careful never to "sell" Jesus to others because "Jesus works." Our task is to share Jesus with others because He is the truth.

The faith Paul reveals to us in this pivotal passage in Romans is dynamic, three-dimensional faith. Let's examine each of the three dimensions of authentic biblical faith—mind, heart, and will—in turn:

1. *Authentic biblical faith must touch the mind.*

I recall the contrast I experienced in the early 1970s when I moved from my home in the Midwest to the cosmopolitan atmosphere of the University of London. I was a philosophy major, and I was surrounded by young men and women who were filled with the cynicism and despair of modern existentialism. It was there that I truly learned to treasure the realistic, objective truth of the Christian gospel. Where else but in biblical Christianity do we find a world view that realistically depicts the wretched state of humanity enslaved by sin, yet that gives us a valid hope for the future? What other world view, religion, or philosophy avoids the extremes of both naive, optimistic humanism and pessimistic, meaningless existentialism? The Christianity of Romans 1, 2, and 3 stands completely alone among a myriad of competing world views in that it encompasses both the horror and the hope of our humanity in a single breathtaking expanse.

Unfortunately, many Christians have lost sight of the objective basis of their faith, and have fallen into the anti-rational mood of the surrounding culture. They preach a Christianity based on feelings or on an irrational "leap of faith." Have we forgotten that Jesus said that the greatest commandment is, "Love the Lord your God with all your heart and with all your soul and with all your *mind*" (Matthew 22:37)? As we approach our faith, do we truly love and honor God with our minds?

I'm not suggesting that all Christians should be academics or intellectuals. I'm simply suggesting that, as Os Guinness has said, "We need to learn to think Christianly." We need to subject every issue to the clarity and purity of Scripture. We need to reasonably, rationally examine our values and ideas in the crystalline light of God's Word.

During the troubled decades of the 1960s and '70s, the Christian philosopher Francis Schaeffer opened his home in Switzerland as a retreat center for young people. As a result, hundreds of young adults, many of whom were experiencing a crisis in their faith, came to this haven called L'Abri. They questioned Schaeffer intensely about the Christian faith: What are the essential truths of Christianity? How can I know it's true? How do I deal with my doubts?

Schaeffer noted that the overwhelming majority of these young inquirers were not from unbelieving backgrounds, but from Christian homes. Tragically, they had grown up in an environment where they were told, "Just believe, don't question." When they reached a point where their doubts and questions could not be denied, their upbringing made them feel guilty about their doubts. They had to make a pilgrimage halfway around the world to find someone who would tell them it was okay to ask questions, that there is no contradiction between faith and reason.

If only more young people had doubted a cult leader named Jim Jones. If only People's Temple members had tested his teaching against the light of Scripture. Those who were not caught in the mass murder-suicide in Jonestown, Guyana, reported that a central command of this cult was, "Don't ask questions, just believe." The people of Jonestown believed sincerely and they were sincerely wrong. Their faith deceived them and killed them.

Malcolm Muggeridge once said, "In order to believe greatly, one must doubt greatly." This sounds like a contradiction, but Muggeridge is absolutely correct. Doubt serves a positive function in refining our faith, in stripping away error. Our ability to reason and doubt is a God-given ability, designed to prevent us from falling prey to such destructive belief systems as the People's Temple and other cults. In a world that offers such an array of philosophies and religions, it is not merely important to believe, it is crucial that we believe *the truth*. Authentic faith must touch the mind.

2. *Authentic biblical faith must touch the heart.*

Again, we return to Jesus' statement that the greatest commandment is, "Love the Lord your God with all your heart and with all your soul and with all your mind." Do you and I truly love and honor God with our hearts? The "heart," as it is understood in Scripture, is that part of the human personality that loves, cares for, reaches out to, and touches others. It's the *feeling* dimension of our humanity.

Faith cannot be lived out in isolation. A purely cerebral, intellectual faith is not really faith at all. It is simply a mental concept. Authentic biblical faith hungers for fellowship and community with other believers. People of authentic faith yearn to reach out to one another and grow together in faith and love.

In recent decades, our society has seen the rise of hundreds of cults, many of which offer a counterfeit version of the heart dimension of faith. As Alvin Toffler observes in *The Third Wave*,

> For lonely people, cults offer . . . indiscriminate friendship. Says an official of the Unification Church: "If someone's lonely, we talk to them. There are a lot of lonely people walking around." The newcomer is surrounded by people offering friendship and beaming approval . . . . So powerfully rewarding is this sudden warmth and attention that

cult members are often willing to give up contact
with their families and former friends, [and] to
donate their life's earnings to the cult.[1]

The travesty and tragedy of the cults is that they
offer the "heart-dimension" without the "head-
dimension." The "faith" of the cults is long on
emotional content, community, love, and acceptance.
But it lacks the rational content of objective truth.

Our task as biblical Christians is to keep the rational
and emotional dimensions of our faith—the "head" and
the "heart"—in balance. A "faith" without reason is a
"faith" unrooted in objective reality. Yet "faith" that is
disconnected from the emotional fabric of close
Christian community and fellowship is equally
distorted. God has not called us to be a loose collection
of "Lone Ranger Christians" but a unified family of
faith. Authentic faith must touch the heart.

3. *Authentic biblical faith must touch the will.*

The will is that part of faith that propels us into
action. Authentic faith calls us to make a decision, to
take a stand, to move out in service to Jesus Christ. The
will-dimension of faith might be viewed as the catalyst
that brings both mind and heart together in a chemical
reaction that erupts in meaningful activity for God.

In Romans 4, Paul returns to the Old Testament to
amplify his teaching on faith. Paul chooses as his
exemplar of faith the patriarch Abraham. As we look
with Paul at the life of Abraham, we find a man who
demonstrated faith by *actions*. Abraham was willing to
uproot himself from his ancestral home and follow the
will of God to a place he didn't know. He was even
willing to sacrifice his own son, if God so ordered, to be
obedient to God.

It is in the will-dimension of faith that there is much misunderstanding in the contemporary church. Many Christian speakers and writers are telling their listeners that "faith" is a device for getting us out of our problems. "Just believe" they say, "and God will take away your sickness, or your financial problems, or your marital problems." But as you examine the Bible and Christian history, you quickly find this is not the case. When faith touches the will, it often gets us into—not out of—trouble.

Can you imagine how the apostle Paul would react to the kind of "feel-good faith" that is preached in so many quarters today? Can you just picture his response—after having endured stonings, beatings, sickness, deprivation, hunger, and shipwreck—to a gospel that says, "Just believe, and God will take away all your problems"? It was Paul's faith, working in the active dimension of his will, that kept getting Paul into trouble time after time!

In *The Screwtape Letters*, C. S. Lewis pictures a dialogue between the senior devil Screwtape and his nephew Wormwood. It is Wormwood's task to derail the faith of his Christian "patient." Screwtape advises, "No amount of piety in his imagination and affections will harm us if we can keep it out of his will."[2] "Faith" that does not issue into action scarcely deserves to be called "faith" at all.

One of the acquaintances of Mark Twain was a notoriously unscrupulous businessman. One evening, this businessman visited Twain at his stately Hartford, Connecticut, home. Over dinner, he boasted of some recent business deals and personal conquests. He gleefully recounted how he had ruined competitors, bribed a prominent politician, and had an affair with a society matron. After dinner, they retired to Twain's study for brandy and cigars. "You know," said the businessman, waxing philosophical, "there's one thing I intend to do before I die. I want to make a pilgrimage to the Holy Land."

"Oh?" said Twain, raising an eyebrow. "Why is that?"

"I want to climb to the top of Mount Sinai and stand on the very spot where the Lord gave the stone tablets to Moses. There I will face the heavens and recite aloud the Ten Commandments."

"Commendable idea," said Twain with a wry smile. "But I have a better one. Why not stay in town and *keep* the Commandments?"

Faith must not only touch the mind and the heart, but the will. The good news of Romans 3 is that we have all the faith we will ever need if we simply place our trust in the great faithfulness of God.

Chapter 7

Rejoicing in Suffering
(Romans 5)

Elaine sat down in my office and opened her Bible to Romans 5. Her husband had died a few weeks earlier. After thirty years of marriage, Elaine was completely alone. Her children were grown and living in distant cities. She spent her days as a cashier in a retail store. Every night, she went home alone, fixed dinner, and laid out place settings for two. And each night as she sat down to eat, she would look across the table at the empty place setting and realize that there would be only one, not two, at the dinner table, that night and every night.

"So Ron," Elaine said as she opened her Bible and placed her finger on Romans 5:3, "I'd like you to explain something to me. What in the world does this mean when it says, 'We rejoice in our sufferings'?"

Not long after that, I officiated a very unusual dedication service for a little baby boy named Danny. What made this dedication unusual is that it took place not in a church sanctuary, but in a hospital room. Danny was seven months old, and throughout his brief life he had been very sick. I prayed and sang hymns with Danny's parents and some close Christian friends. We laughed and cried together, and we dedicated this fragile little life to the Lord.

A few days later, I officiated a second service for Danny. This time it was a memorial service. Afterwards, I spent time in the home of Danny's parents. Their arms were empty. Their only child was with Jesus now. And as we were talking together, Danny's father said, "The other day, I read a verse in Romans that said, 'We rejoice in our sufferings.' In light of what we have been through for the past seven months, and what we are going through right now, that seems like such a strange thing to say. Does God expect us to rejoice even in this?"

These are hard questions, realistic questions, and they are voiced by those who are in the trenches of life. Because suffering is an inevitable dimension of this life, you and I need a strategy for suffering. As we examine Paul's teaching on suffering as it is embedded in the flow of Romans, we find he offers us precisely what we seek: a practical strategy for life's hard places. In Romans 5:1–5, he writes:

> Therefore, since we have been justified through faith, we have peace with God through our Lord Jesus Christ, through whom we have gained access by faith into this grace in which we now stand. And we rejoice in the hope of the glory of God. Not only so but we also rejoice in our sufferings, because we know that suffering produces perseverance; perseverance, character; and character, hope. And hope does not disappoint us, because God has poured out his love into our hearts by the Holy Spirit, whom he has given us.

Notice in this passage that Paul never tells us to rejoice *for* our suffering, as many Christians mistakenly teach these days. There is a big difference between rejoicing *because* we are suffering and rejoicing *in* our suffering. Paul is not suggesting that we should be masochistic, that we should take some sort of perverse pleasure in our suffering. Nor is Paul teaching stoicism, a kind of "grin-and-bear-it" indifference to the pain of suffering. Nor is Paul advocating fatalism, the resignation of oneself to a horrible fate.

When Paul writes, "but we also rejoice in our sufferings," he is laying the foundation for a bold strategy for transforming suffering into a benefit in our lives and the lives of others. Moreover, Paul does not proclaim this strategy alone and in isolation from the rest of Scripture. His message echoes that of Jesus, who said, "Blessed are those who mourn, for they will be comforted . . . . Blessed are you when people insult you, persecute you and falsely say all kinds of evil against you because of me. Rejoice and be glad, because great is your reward in heaven . . ." (Matthew 5:4, 11–12). Paul's message also echoes that of Peter: "Dear friends, do not be surprised at the painful trial you are suffering, as though something strange were happening to you. But rejoice that you participate in the sufferings of Christ, so that you may be overjoyed when his glory is revealed" (1 Peter 4:12–13). Paul also echoes the counsel of James: "Consider it pure joy, my brothers, whenever you face trials of many kinds, because you know that the testing of your faith develops perseverance" (James 1:2–3).

And the point that Jesus, Peter, James, and Paul are getting at is this: Suffering has a purpose. Suffering has an explanation. Suffering has the power to produce positive benefits in our lives. We can rejoice in suffering because suffering produces something valuable:

perseverance—the ability to endure under pressure.

Paul goes on to say that perseverance produces character, and character is the pivotal term in this passage. In the original Greek, this word translated "character" is *dokimos*, literally meaning "tested and approved." Suffering produces perseverance, and perseverance produces proven character.

If you travel in the Middle East, you will probably find pottery shops that sell earthen vessels with the word *dokimos* inscribed on the bottom. This means the vessel has gone through the fire, it has been tested, and it has come out without breaking or cracking. So the potter stamps it *dokimos*, approved. Like that vessel, you and I go through the furnace of testing, and when we have emerged unbroken, with our character refined by fire, we have earned the stamp of God's *dokimos*, His approval.

Paul then goes on to say that character produces hope. Throughout the flow of the New Testament, we see that *hope* refers to our expectation as we look forward to the future, and to the certainty of spending eternity with Jesus Christ. As Paul will later say in Romans 8:18, "I consider that our present sufferings are not worth comparing with the glory that will be revealed in us." Remember that Paul is writing these words to Christians living under the capricious and oppressive rule of Nero. There is nothing glib or trite about his counsel.

Now we have the basis of Paul's strategy for suffering. It's a three-point strategy, so let's examine the three biblical principles that emerge from Romans 5:1–5.

1. *We rejoice in our suffering because suffering enables us to identify with Christ.* Whether we like it or not, we have to acknowledge that there is no other

point in life where we feel more closely identified with
our Lord Jesus than in a time of suffering. Again and
again in my own times of trial, I go back to Isaiah 53:4,
which says, "Surely he took up our infirmities and
carried our sorrows." Clearly, Jesus identified with you
and me, taking on our humanity with all its suffering
and pain. And as we in turn undergo times of suffering,
we experience a closeness to Jesus that we find at no
other time in our lives. That's why Paul, in Philippians
3:10, says, "I want to know Christ and the power of His
resurrection and the fellowship of sharing in his
sufferings, becoming like him in his death."

Several years ago, I lost a close friend and spiritual
counselor to cancer. During the last few weeks of his
life, he became thin, dehydrated, and very weak. He lost
control of his bodily functions. During one of my visits
to his hospital room, I grasped his hand and he looked
up at me and said, "Ron, these days I feel identified
with Christ in ways I've never understood before. I have
just a taste of the hurt and humiliation He must have
felt as He hung on the cross, hour after hour. I feel
closer to Jesus right now than ever before."

There are many churches and many Christian
speakers these days who are teaching that Jesus came
and suffered to remove our suffering, to make us healthy
and wealthy. As I have read the Bible and lived out my
own pilgrimage with God and watched the lives of other
Christians, I have come to a very different conclusion.
I'm convinced that Christ did *not* die so that we would
never have to suffer. Rather, Christ died so that *our*
suffering would be like *His*. And what was the suffering
of Jesus like? It was purposeful. It was meaningful. It
was sacrificial. Jesus suffered for the benefit of others,

so that people like you and me might truly live.

We must realistically face the fact that there will be struggle in our lives. There will be pain. But our pain is no longer meaningless. Our pain has been transformed. It is like the pain of Jesus Himself.

2. *We rejoice in our suffering because we know that suffering produces character.* We must be careful to avoid the false teaching found in many corners of Christendom that, through the death of Christ, suffering has been nullified or that suffering has been rendered less difficult for the Christian or that suffering is caused by some sin or spiritual deficiency. No, godly Christians suffer just as non-Christians do, in equal proportions and to an equal degree. The difference is that the Christian understands that his or her suffering is producing something of eternal value: refined, approved character. When you emerge from the fire of your trial—whether in this life or the life to come—you emerge with God's stamp of *dokimos* on your life. You are a man or woman approved by God.

Paul understood this principle. As we study his life we see that the more he suffered for Jesus Christ, the more he grew in character. Through his trials, Paul could trust the fact that the hand of God is sure and steady, no matter how hot the furnace, no matter how intense the pain. Paul knew he could trust the faithfulness of God even at the brink of the ultimate trial of human character, death itself. I want that kind of character.

Deep down, we all want to be people of character. The problem most of us have is that we're accustomed to easy solutions and instant gratification. We want character, but we don't want the suffering. We want the product, but we don't want the process.

The hard fact is that the process—suffering—is inevitable in this life. The only choice we have is whether or not we will adopt an attitude of openness to what God wants to teach us through suffering. We have to choose whether or not to allow the process of suffering to bring forth the product of character. Refined, approved character is not built in an ivory tower. It is built in the trenches.

3. *We rejoice in our suffering because we know that suffering gives us the opportunity to minister to others.* In Romans 5:5, Paul writes, "God has poured out His love into our hearts by the Holy Spirit, whom he has given us." In times of suffering, God's love breaks through and touches our hearts, giving us a passion to take the pain that has come into our lives, and to use it as a source of healing for others.

Consider this: Who is in a better position to comfort a grieving parent than someone who has endured the hurt of such a loss? Who can better understand the needs of an alcoholic who has hit bottom than someone who has been to the bottom and back? Who can better touch the hurts of someone going through a divorce, a business failure, the heartbreak of a rebellious teenager, or a struggle with self-esteem than someone who has been there and has felt God's healing touch there?

God is calling you and me to become wounded healers, offering our suffering to God, allowing Him to transform our hurts into healing ministry to others.

You probably know of Elisabeth Elliot, and the story of how her missionary husband Jim Elliot was martyred for Jesus Christ by the Auca tribe in Ecuador. But perhaps you did not know that she was later remarried to a man named Addison Leitch. Addison was a close friend of our family during the years I was growing up in Iowa. He was also the vice-president of the college from which I graduated. Shortly after Elisabeth Elliott married Addison Leitch, he was diagnosed with a rare form of cancer. Elisabeth was required to care for her husband literally day and night, while watching him suffer incredible agonies from his cancer.

In the beginning, she would pray for the strength to get through the week. Then the task became so difficult she would pray for the strength to get through the day. It finally got to the point where she would just ask God for the strength to get through the hour because at 9:00 A.M. it was inconceivable that she would be able to endure until 10:00 A.M.

During one of those rare moments of rest and respite, Elisabeth reread the story in John 6 where Jesus took the five loaves and two fish offered by a little boy. Blessing and breaking the boy's meager offering, Jesus was able to transform it and feed a multitude. "That," Elisabeth realized, "is what Jesus wants to do with my trial right now."

That is what Jesus wants to do with your trial as well. As you and I in faith offer our suffering to Jesus, He is able to bless it, break it, transform it, and use it to feed a multitude. Whether your suffering seems great or small, God can turn it into healing for others.

Even in our times of hardship and heartbreak, we know that we are finding greater identification with Christ, proven character, and the opportunity to reach out in love to others. Trusting in the great faithfulness of God, we rejoice in the hope of the glory to come, and we realistically rejoice—even in our sufferings.

Chapter 8

Dead to Sin
(Romans 6)

Her first thought was, *I'm blacking out*! The kitchen of her apartment seemed to reel and shake. Her knees buckled and she tumbled to the floor a few feet from where her four-year-old daughter was playing. Then she realized there was nothing wrong with her. The apartment really *was* shaking. The walls were dancing. Plaster was crumbling. Suddenly, there was the sickening sensation of weightlessness, as if she were in a free-falling elevator. The room cracked and splintered. "Gayaney!" she cried out, clutching at her terrified little girl.

In a few seconds, it was over. The first shock of the December 1988 earthquake in Soviet Armenia had struck. The thirty-six story apartment building in which Susanna Petrosyan and her four-year-old daughter Gayaney lived had been reduced to a mound of rubble. From the top to the bottom of Susanna's building, ceilings had pancaked onto floors, killing scores of her neighbors. But Susanna and her daughter were spared—spared yet buried alive. They were sandwiched in an eighteen-inch gap between the floor and the collapsed ceiling.

For the first few hours of their ordeal, Susanna lay on her back, trying to quiet her daughter's fears. Aware of the enormous pile of debris that covered them, Susanna despaired of ever being rescued in time. Yet she refused to give up the struggle for life—especially her daughter's life. Wriggling painfully in her confined space, groping for food or water, her fingers found an object of hope: a half-empty jar of fruit jam. With her fingers, she fed the jam to Gayaney.

Gayaney was quiet for a while, then Susanna heard her weakly plead, "Mamma, I'm thirsty."

There was no water. "Hush," said Susanna. "Rest. Wait." Time passed.

"Mamma," Gayaney whimpered again, "Mamma, I'm thirsty."

Night came, then day, then night again. There was no more food, no water, no help. By this time, Gayaney had become too weak to plead for water. Afraid that her little girl would die of dehydration, Susanna did the only thing she could think of. She broke the empty jar and used a shard of glass to slit her finger. Then she placed her bleeding finger in Gayaney's mouth.

Again and again, Susanna repeated this process, sustaining her daughter's life with her own blood.

Eight days. Eight days of claustrophobic horror, boredom, hunger, and thirst. Finally Susanna's husband and rescue workers clawed their way into the narrow space where Susanna and Gayaney were entombed. Susanna had not only conquered her ordeal, but she had kept her little girl alive with the sacrifice of her own blood.

This story is a parable of Paul's message to us in Romans 6. Just as little Gayaney was buried alive with her mother and sustained day by day on her mother's precious lifeblood, so Paul tells us that we are buried with Christ, and we are raised to life by the shedding of His precious lifeblood. In Romans 6:1–4, Paul writes:

What shall we say, then? Shall we go on sinning so that grace may increase? By no means! We died to sin; how can we live in it any longer? Or don't you know that all of us who were baptized into Christ Jesus were baptized into his death? We were therefore buried with him through baptism into death in order that, just as Christ was raised from the dead through the glory of the Father, we too may live a new life.

You are alive in Christ and dead to sin. This is Paul's theme in Romans 6. Sin is a concept that has fallen sharply out of favor in our culture. We live in a society that not only tolerates sin but celebrates it in books, films, music, television, and the lifestyles of our stars and heroes. We are barraged by the most pervasive array of influences and temptations of any age in human history. So Paul's message becomes all the more relevant and urgent to you and me as we struggle to live after the example of Christ in this post-Christian age of the 1990s.

In this passage, Paul anticipates an attitude that has infected the thinking of many secularized Christians in our age. It is the attitude that says, "Whatever I do, God will forgive me. I know His grace will cover my sin, so I'll live however I please."

Paul's answer to such an attitude is more than emphatic: It fairly *shouts* from the page, "By no means!" (The King James Version cries out, "God forbid!," and J. B. Phillips translation is even more pungent: "What a ghastly thought!") Paul then amplifies this vehement retort with a series of shocking

word-images: We were *buried* with Christ, verse 4. Our
old self has been *crucified*, verse 6. We should count
ourselves *dead* to sin, verse 11. We were formerly
slaves to sin; now we are to live as *slaves to God*, verses
20 and 22.

Strong images. We are unaccustomed to viewing
ourselves and our condition in such stark terms. Yet if
we are to truly become whole people in this broken
world, we urgently need to grasp God's view of sin, and
Paul's strategy for dealing with temptation.

Temptation surrounds us in this money-mad, fast-
track, success-oriented world. Perhaps the most
surprising dynamic of temptation is that the problem of
temptation seems to actually increase rather than
decrease as we become more successful and financially
secure. As F. B. Meyer insightfully observed, "We may
expect temptation in days of prosperity and ease rather
than in those of privation and toil . . . . Not when the
youth is climbing arduously the step ladder of fame, but
when he has attained the golden portals; not where men
frown, but where they smile sweet exquisite smiles of
flattery—it is *there* that the temptress lies in waiting!
Beware! If you go armed anywhere, you must, above all,
go armed there."[1] Those words were written nearly a
century ago, and they were never truer than they are
today.

The principle that growing success brings greater
temptation is exemplified by the life of Joseph in the
book of Genesis. After being sold into slavery by his
jealous brothers, Joseph found success, achievement,
and promotion in the employ of his Egyptian slave-
master, Potiphar. He was placed in charge of Potiphar's
entire household, and with that promotion came

temptation at its most intense. The source of Joseph's temptation was his master's wife, who wantonly offered her sexual favors to Joseph. Day after day she pursued Joseph, and day after day this young man clung to his integrity as she cajoled, then insisted, then threatened, and finally *forced* herself on him. To escape temptation, Joseph finally had to physically *flee* the temptress and remove himself from the situation.

I've known a number of people whom I consider contemporary Josephs. I'm reminded of the young athletes I knew when I was a Bible teacher for the Minnesota Vikings. Like Joseph, who is described in Genesis 39:6 as "well-built and handsome," pro-football players are virile, broad-shouldered, good-looking guys who enjoy the adulation of the fans, the praise of the media, and the attention of beautiful young women. They are paid huge sums of money and attain national fame.

I especially remember one player coming to me after a road trip. "You know, Ron," he said, "we arrived in Detroit on Saturday evening for the game on Sunday. As I walked to my hotel room, outside the door was a line of beautiful young women waiting just for me. I could have taken my pick." That's the kind of temptation that often comes with power and success.

Joseph may have been a high-ranking slave in the household of Potiphar, but he obeyed an even higher Master than Potiphar. Joseph seemed to intuitively anticipate Paul's admonition in Romans 6:16–18:

> Don't you know that . . . you are slaves to the one whom you obey—whether you are slaves to sin, which leads to death, or to obedience, which leads to righteousness? But thanks be to God that,

though you used to be slaves to sin, you
wholeheartedly obeyed the form of teaching to
which you were entrusted. You have been set free
from sin and have become slaves to righteousness.

That was Joseph—a slave to righteousness. And
because Joseph saw God as his ultimate Master, he was
empowered to stand up to the pressure and temptation
of sexual harassment from his employer's wife.

Joseph never had to deal with such temptation when he
was just another one of his master's many slaves. But with
promotion comes prestige. And with prestige, all too often
comes pride. Joseph did not succumb to the pride and
temptation that has toppled so many twentieth-century
leaders into scandal and disgrace. Joseph found the words
of F. B. Meyer to be true: "We may expect temptation in
days of prosperity and ease . . . ." It's sobering to realize
that the "prosperity and ease" that came to Joseph are
paltry compared to the riches, the leisure pursuits, and the
technological wonders that are available to the most
ordinary middle-class wage-earner today.

Our society has become a smorgasboard of alluring
temptations. Hard-core pornography, which used to be
confined to the sleaziest sections of our cities, is now
within easy reach of every American home. In almost
every video rental store, all you have to do is stroll past
the current comedies and adventure films, the racks of
Disney titles and video-game cartridges, and there
under the glass counter is "the blue catalog"—a thick
compilation of the most lurid and explicit sex and
violence films ever made. These same films are
available at the touch of a button on many metropolitan
cable systems, in many hotel rooms, and even on your
own family's TV set if you own a satellite dish.

But sexual temptation is just one of the spiritual dangers we face in the 1990s. You may be tempted to fudge on your taxes or cut ethical corners in your business. You may be tempted to use power, influence, and money to impose your will on others or to demand your way in the church. You may have a problem with gossip, anger, or profanity. You may be so bent on acquiring wealth, status, and possessions that you are neglecting your family. Your problem may be a lack of truthfulness or faithfulness to your promises. These temptations are common to us all, regardless of our station in life.

Whatever your area of temptation, it's time to get serious about dying to that sin. It's time to throw off your yoke of enslavement to temptation and begin truly living as a slave to righteousness. Let me suggest to you a three-point strategy for dealing with temptation.

1. *Flee temptation.* "Flee the evil desires of youth," wrote Paul to his spiritual son Timothy, "and pursue righteousness, faith, love and peace" (2 Tim. 2:22). What does it mean to "flee" from sin? Returning to Joseph in the Old Testament, we find one way to flee temptation: Put one foot in front of the other and *run*. When Potiphar's wife attempted to force herself on Joseph, he broke away from her grasp so hastily that she was still clutching his cloak as he made his getaway.

Do you and I go to such lengths to avoid entanglement with sin? Do we, like Joseph, like Paul, consider ourselves dead to sin and slaves of righteousness? If we're honest, we have to admit that we probably tend to flirt with sin more than we flee it.

We human beings have an amazing capacity for self-deception. We pretend to ourselves that we have repented, that we have died to our old sins—yet there is a sneaking part of us that keeps the door open to sin . . . just a crack. And that little crack is all sin needs to get a foot in the door of our lives.

Ed is addicted to pornography. For years, he has kept a secret stash of pornographic magazines hidden around the house. And he has a habit of calling pornographic phone services late at night, after his wife, Mary, goes to bed. For a long time, he kept his addiction hidden from his wife by keeping his magazines hidden and making sure she never saw the phone bills.

One day Mary came across his magazines while cleaning house. When Ed came home from work, the magazines were fanned out on the dining room table. Mary sat at the table with tears in her eyes. "Why, Ed?" she said in a voice filled with hurt and disappointment. "And what else has been going on that I don't know about?"

Ed hesitated, then sighed deeply. "There is something else," he said, and in a halting voice he told her about the late-night toll calls. "I've run up a phone bill of over a thousand dollars. We can't pay it. The phone company's going to cut us off next week."

Mary was silent for a long time. "Ed," she said at last, "if we can't have complete trust and honesty between us, I can't stay here. I'm leaving you—unless . . ."

"Unless what?"

"Unless you get some counseling. Unless we both go into counseling together."

Ed agreed. The following week they sat in the counselor's office. His cheeks burning with shame, Ed poured out the story of his addiction in front of his wife and the counselor. "I've really struggled with this temptation," he concluded. "I've fought it and fought it."

"How did you fight it?" asked the counselor.

"I tried to summon the willpower not to open one of those magazines, or not to dial that number."

"Did you ever just throw the magazines in the trash? Did you ever simply get rid of them?" asked the counselor. "Or did you ever call the phone company and ask that your access to those phone numbers be blocked? Surely these options must have occurred to you."

Ed stared at the floor, unable to meet the counselor's eyes. "Yes," he sighed. "I thought of doing those things. But I couldn't bring myself to do anything so . . . final."

Part of Ed's problem was that he flirted with temptation rather than fleeing from it. While telling himself he was "struggling" with his addiction and "fighting" temptation, he had been keeping the door open all along. Until Ed admitted the truth to himself, he was doomed to be a slave to sin.

Your temptation may be different from Ed's, but the principle is the same. There are times when we are strong, when temptation has no hold on us. And there are other times when the temptation we faced so bravely before now looms over us as an irresistible force. We need to take steps in those strong moments— those moments when we are thinking clearly and biblically about temptation—to build barriers between ourselves and sin, to remove the sources of temptation from our lives. This is what it means to "flee temptation."

2. *Build integrity into your life.* Some synonyms for *integrity* might be *wholeness*, *congruence*, and *consistency*. To have integrity means to have no contradiction between our inner actions and the image

of ourselves that we project to others. It means that you don't pretend to be something you are not.

Another dimension of Ed's losing battle with temptation was his lack of consistency between his secret inner life and the outer image he was maintaining. He was living a lie before outsiders and before his own wife. Moreover, he was lying to himself, telling himself he was "fighting" temptation when all along he was really accommodating to it.

Many people have been devastated by a great sin because they have lacked integrity in lesser issues. If a person in business has so much integrity that he or she does not even take home a single paper clip belonging to the company, then you can bet that person will never be caught fudging the expense account or lying to the IRS. If a person avoids profane language in those secret, unguarded moments when nobody is watching, then such words will never accidentally escape at an embarrassing moment. When we have integrity in the small things, then we insure ourselves against succumbing to larger temptations.

3. *Build mutually accountable relationships with others.* We all need a few friends who will love us enough to listen to our hurts and struggles without judging us, who will check on our spiritual progress and hold us accountable for our growth, who will pray for us and be available to us when we are in need. I've found the best way to build relationships is through small fellowship groups that are built around Bible study, prayer, and open sharing. Many churches have such groups as part of the life of the congregation.

From his vantage in the news business, columnist Cal Thomas has seen scores of lives—politicians, business leaders, and religious leaders—ruined by the lure of temptation. The reputations and careers of these individuals could have been saved if they had made themselves accountable for their lifestyle. Thomas told an interviewer for *Discipleship Journal*:

> Regardless of our role or status, we need to be accountable to others who lovingly ask us hard questions about our goals and motivations and hold us true to our faith in Jesus Christ . . . . This usually happens most effectively within a small group where people have made commitments to one another and established trust . . . . Each of us needs that small group of Christians who love us, pray for us, know us, encourage us, correct us—who help us remain true in our pursuit of the godly life.[1]

Some years ago, a Christian social worker—fresh out of college—was working in a poor area of a large industrial city. There she came to know a boy who was badly crippled. His body was so bent and deformed that he was unable to stand or to sit. He could only huddle in a curled position.

The social worker investigated this little boy's history and found he had been injured in an accident several months earlier. He had been hit by a car while chasing a ball in the street. His parents were very poor and uninformed about how to obtain government assistance for their child's medical care. So they had simply picked up their child, wrapped him in a blanket, and placed him in bed. His bones mended incorrectly, leaving the boy severely crippled.

The social worker made this boy her own special project. She helped him get the medical treatment he needed. Over a period of several years he underwent sixteen operations to correct his deformities. Eventually, he was able to walk and run and play like any other child.

Years later, the woman stood before a convention of social workers and told the story of this little boy and how he had been healed of his deformities. Then she said, "I lost touch with that little boy for several years, and I often wondered where he was and what he was doing, now that he's grown to be a young man. A few days ago, I found out. Would any of you care to guess what my young friend is doing now?"

Various people in the audience ventured guesses. "Has he gone into social work?" No. "Perhaps he's a politician?" No. "A pastor?" No. "A teacher?" No.

"No," she said, her eyes glistening, "he never went on to achieve the things I wished for when I first saw that crippled little boy. Today, he's sitting on death row, in a prison not far from here. That little boy grew up to become a murderer. You see, we taught him *how* to walk—but we never showed him *where* to walk."

The good news of Romans 6 is that Jesus not only showed us how to walk. He not only raised us from death to life. He also showed us where to walk. He has called us to walk in righteousness, to walk in the light. Though we used to be slaves to sin, we have been set free to live as slaves to righteousness. As Paul exultantly expresses at the conclusion of Romans 6, "But now that you have been set free from sin and have become slaves to God, the benefit you reap leads to holiness, and the result is eternal life. For the wages of sin is death, but the gift of God is eternal life in Christ Jesus our Lord."

Chapter 9

— *The Christian Struggle* —
(Romans 7)

In his *Confessions*, Saint Augustine describes the sinful and rebellious life he led as a young man, and how his life was changed by his conversion to Jesus Christ. Yet, even as he was on his knees, praying his prayer of remorse and repentance to God, there was an inner struggle going on, for the words of his prayer were, "Lord Jesus, give me chastity and self-control—but not yet."

Newspaperman Don Marquis knew how Augustine felt. Marquis, the author of the famous "Archy and Mehitabel" stories, struggled for years with an alcohol problem. Finally he resolved to "go on the wagon," to stop drinking altogether. Day by day, he fought his thirst for that one glass of gin that would be his undoing. In time he became so irritable his friends were afraid to be around him. Finally, after being "dry" an entire month, Marquis walked into one of his old "watering holes" and ordered a double martini.

"Gee, Mr. Marquis," said the startled bartender, "I haven't seen you in weeks! I thought you were through with this stuff!"

"I was, Johnnie," Marquis replied, lifting the glass to his lips. "I had a long argument with myself about this drink—and I finally conquered my willpower."

Perhaps you can identify with the inner struggle of young Augustine and of Don Marquis. You probably know what it feels like to be a walking battlefield, your conflicting desires at war within you. I certainly know that feeling, and as we come to Romans 7, we discover that Paul knew that feeling, too. In verses 14 through 25, he writes:

> We know that the law is spiritual; but I am unspiritual, sold as a slave to sin. I do not understand what I do. For what I want to do I do not do, but what I hate I do. And if I do what I do not want to do, I agree that the law is good. As it is, it is no longer I myself who do it, but it is sin living in me. I know that nothing good lives in me, that is, in my sinful nature. For I have the desire to do what is good, but I cannot carry it out. For what I do is not the good I want to do; no, the evil I do not want to do—this I keep on doing. Now if I do what I do not want to do, it is no longer I who do it, but it is sin living in me that does it.
>
> So I find this law at work: When I want to do good, evil is right there with me. For in my inner being I delight in God's law; but I see another law at work in the members of my body, waging war against the law of my mind and making me a prisoner of the law of sin at work within my members. What a wretched man I am! Who will rescue me from this body of death? Thanks be to God—through Jesus Christ our Lord!
>
> So then, I myself in my mind am a slave to God's law, but in the sinful nature a slave to the law of sin.

In this passage, Paul becomes very personal, transparent, and vulnerable with us. We get to look into the heart of this great man of Christian history.

Many years ago, Karl Marx declared that the key to human history is the class struggle between rich and poor. If the apostle Paul were here today, he would say, "Marx was naive. Yes, there is a class struggle going on, but that's not the fundamental struggle, the root struggle of the human condition. The key to understanding human history is the struggle that rages within the human heart. It's the fact that we want to do good, but evil always strives for mastery within us." Though it is Marx's ideas that are often called "radical," it is actually Paul who is a radical in the truest sense of the word. For the word *radical* comes from the Latin *radix*, meaning "root." And it is Paul, not Marx, who gets to the root of our human condition.

In addition to being a profoundly honest and autobiographical passage, Romans 7 is also a highly controversial passage. Through the centuries, it has puzzled faithful Bible scholars, and this puzzlement has given rise to three different interpretations. Let's look at those interpretations in turn:

First, there are Bible scholars who believe Paul is speaking rhetorically in Romans 7. They suggest that Paul is talking about the way his life was *before* his dramatic conversion to Christ. They believe he is describing the life of a Jew trying to fulfill the law apart from Christ when he writes: "What I want to do I do not do, but what I do I hate." This view has been held by many of the early church fathers, by both Roman Catholic and Protestant pietists, and by such twentieth-century theologians as Emil Brunner and Rudolf Bultmann.

A second interpretation of Romans 7 suggests that Paul is writing about the Christian life after conversion, but before a "second blessing" experience—the baptism or filling of the Holy Spirit. According to this view, there is a second work of grace, which gives Christians instantaneous, supernatural victory over sin. Paul is interpreted as saying, "Yes, there is a struggle in Romans 7, but that struggle will be cancelled out in Romans 8." As we will discover, Romans 8 is a detailed introduction to the Holy Spirit, who is mentioned twenty times in that one chapter. Proponents of this view believe Paul is writing about a struggle that disappears once a Christian is filled and empowered by the Holy Spirit. There are Christians within the charismatic movement, pentacostalism, fundamentalism, and evangelicalism who hold this view. Some of my favorite Bible commentators, such as Charles Eerdman and Kenneth Wuest, hold this view. So if you agree with this interpretation of Romans 7, you are in good company.

The problem I have with the second interpretation is that Paul, in Romans 8:26 writes: "The Spirit helps us in our weakness." Moreover, the Greek word used by Jesus to describe the Holy Spirit in the gospel of John, chapters 14, 15, and 16 is *parakletos,* a word that suggests someone who has come alongside us to aid us in our struggle. It seems clear to me that the flow of Romans, and of the entire New Testament, indicates that the presence of the Holy Spirit in no way cancels out the reality of our human struggle. The struggle goes on, yet the Holy Spirit, the Parakletos, is alongside us in our weakness, helping us through our struggle.

So while many sincere, knowledgeable Christians have come to other conclusions regarding Romans 7, I believe a third view is better supported by the text of Romans 7 and the context of the New Testament. According to this third view, Paul is writing about an ever-present, daily struggle in the life of Spirit-filled, committed Christians. I come to this conclusion because Paul, who is an educated, precise, and eloquent writer, uses verb tenses in this passage that refer to his life at the present time.

Paul does not say, "This is the way life was before I received Christ." He does not say, "This is the way life was before God's second work of grace in my life." The plainest sense of Paul's words is, "Right now, as a redeemed, born-again, Spirit-filled Christian, my life is a struggle. I want to do good, but there is a part of me that wants to do evil." Nowhere in this chapter do I find anything abstract, theoretical, or metaphorical. Rather, I find an honest confession of a continual and painful spiritual reality.

This view of Romans 7 was supported by the early reformers, Martin Luther and John Calvin, and continues to be espoused by contemporary commentators such as Ray Stedman, Earl Palmer, John Stott, F. F. Bruce, and William Barclay. These Bible scholars all conclude that Paul is telling us that we live out our Christian lives, from our conversion until the moment of our death, in a struggle. I believe these scholars come to this conclusion not only because the flow of the text and Paul's use of verb tenses support it, but because this interpretation matches the experience of their own lives. It certainly matches my experience. I suspect it matches yours as well.

I believe what Paul is clearly telling us in this passage is that all the days of our lives will be lived out in a struggle between our two selves, between the evil that is inherent in our fallen nature and the good that seeks in obedience to be conformed to the image of Jesus Christ. It's a tough struggle. Sometimes it's a painful struggle. But it's a *good* struggle. And Paul wants us to realize that it's not a struggle to be feared, but to be understood and accepted.

How, then, do we fight the good Christian battle to live in obedience before God? Before answering the question, let me suggest two *mistaken* solutions to this struggle:

The first false answer to the Christian struggle is, "Reduce the cost of obedience." There are voices in the Christian church today saying that if we could just reduce the cost of Christian discipleship, if we could just make the Christian message a little more accommodating, a little less demanding, then the struggle would be diminished and Christianity would be more attractive. If we could just allow Jesus to be Savior without making Him Lord, then we would diminish the struggle. Such a view treats the Christian faith as a convenient "fire escape," a passport out of hell, without altering anyone's life or behavior in the here and now.

Ironically, this false "solution" to the Christian struggle does not increase the appeal of Christianity. In reality, when you reduce the *cost* of following Christ, you reduce the *appeal* of following Christ as well. Scores of empty, dying churches have discovered this truth too late. When a church reduces the demand of Christian discipleship, it becomes indistinguishable from the broken world around it. In short, it loses its reason for existing. As Jesus says in Matthew 5:13, "If the salt loses its saltiness . . . it is no longer good for anything, except to be thrown out and trampled."

My best sport in high school and college was running. When I was in college, the track coach was actually a man who had been hired to coach basketball.

He really didn't have much interest in track, and when he met with the track team for the first time, he didn't see much potential in us. So this coach reduced the demand of being on the track team. Though practice was scheduled for 4:00 P.M., his advice to us was, "Come out when you can, and work out on your own. If you can't come out to practice, try to get in some running in the evening or in the morning before school. I'm afraid I won't be out here very much, so I've typed up a sheet of suggested workouts for you."

Many of those who had come out for the track team quit in disillusionment after the first meeting. No one wanted to be on a team that made no demands and had no standards. But one of my teammates had an idea. "Why do we have to be on the school track team at all?" he said. "Why don't we form a track *club*? We could coach ourselves. We could motivate and encourage and discipline each other to become the best in the state!"

Calling ourselves the Council Bluffs Striders, we got together and trained. We underwent a tough self-imposed discipline. We couldn't afford the colorful track uniforms of the other schools, so we spray-painted "Council Bluffs Striders" across the chests of our T-shirts. We worked and sweated and pushed ourselves until the day of the Midwest AAU Finals, a huge meet with teams from all the midwestern states, sponsored by the Amateur Athletic Union. When that day was over, our team had finished second in the two-mile relay.

Since then, I've always remembered that when you reduce the demand of involvement, you reduce the appeal of involvement. We must never try to "sell" Christianity to the world by playing down the cost of being a Christian. This is a false solution to the Christian struggle.

A second mistaken solution to the Christian struggle is to teach that a Christian can live above the struggles of life. This has become a very fashionable teaching in certain quarters of Christianity. There are seminar teachers and TV preachers who claim to impart a "secret" to the victorious Christian life—a "secret" by which we can escape such struggles as temptation, loss, grief, pain, illness, and conflict. Such a view is closer to the ancient gnostic heresies and New Age delusions than to biblical Christianity.

Jesus did not come to take us *out* of the struggles of life, but to lead us *through* them. And Jesus has sent us His Holy Spirit to be alongside us, aiding us and strengthening us in the fight. We have a Comforter, an Encourager, a Counselor always at our side—but the struggle of Romans 7 remains with us to a greater or lesser degree throughout all the days of our lives.

So let's return to the question: How do we fight the good Christian battle in obedience to God? We do so in three ways:

First, we must learn to leave room for failure. We should accept the fact that we will fail—and that's okay. I'm sure you're familiar with Christian testimonies that tell how Christ has given someone victory in a troubled marriage, or victory over alcohol, or victory over temptation. And if you're like some Christians I know, you may have grown up feeling a little guilty, a little inadequate, a little bewildered because you continue to struggle in some of these same areas. You don't feel God has given you victory, and you wonder what's wrong with you. Perhaps you've even felt that to be accepted by your Christian friends, you have to pretend to have victory even when you don't. Perhaps you feel you're just a failure, wearing a "victorious Christian" mask.

Romans 7 gives us the freedom to take off our masks, to admit who we are. We have the freedom to admit before others that we've failed, we're struggling, but we're committed to continuing the struggle in the power of the Holy Spirit. Romans 7 gives us the right to say with Paul, "Wretched person that I am! But thanks be to God, Jesus is still Lord and with His help, I'm going to see this struggle through! I still wrestle with my marriage, with feelings of bitterness and anger, with my relationships with others, with temptation—but the Holy Spirit is aiding me in my struggle." That's authentic Christianity.

In this passage, Paul sets for us a beautiful example of honesty, openness, and vulnerability as he shares with us his own inner struggle. It's an example we would do well to emulate. Paul reveals himself as an authentic flesh-and-blood human being, and by his example he gives you and me the right to live before our families and friends as authentic human beings as well.

In my own life, I always make sure that I'm a part of at least one small group of Christians with whom I have the freedom to share my own struggles and failures. There is an enormously healing and transforming power that's released among Christians when they take the risk of sharing their frailty and humanity with others. Certainly, we want to hear those testimonies of authentic victory in the Christian life, but the good news of Romans 7 is that an authentic testimony of how God is bringing us through our hurts and struggles is equally valid.

The second way we respond to the Christian struggle of Romans 7 is by acknowledging that a life without struggle is impossible. That means we have to live realistically.

By living realistically, I don't mean we should live fatalistically. God never intended us to live under a continual cloud, always expecting the worst. Unfortunately, all too many Christians go through life like Eeyore, the sawdust-stuffed donkey in A. A. Milne's fantasy *Winnie-the-Pooh*. We see Eeyore's fatalism when his tail falls off, and his friend Christopher Robin has to tack it back on. "There," says Christopher Robin, "did I get your tail back on properly, Eeyore?" The old gray donkey's morose reply: "No matter. Most likely lose it again anyway." That's not realism; that's pessimism. To live realistically means to live optimistically, yet with the realization that things will sometimes go wrong and temptations must sometimes be faced.

In Hitler's Germany at the height of World War II, the protestant theologian Dietrich Bonhoeffer was in prison for taking an active stand against Hitler. Though imprisoned, Bonhoeffer continued to write and urge those in the Confessing Church to oppose Nazi tyranny, to bring their Christian faith to bear on the injustice of their society, to stand firm, and to endure the trials and persecutions of the time.

During those days, a group of Christians approached Bonhoeffer and tried to dissuade him from being so vocal in his opposition to Naziism. These Christians were deeply interested in Bible prophecy. They believed (understandably) that Hitler was the Antichrist, and that Jesus Christ would return any day. "Why," they asked Bonhoeffer, "do you expose yourself to all this danger and mistreatment by the government? Jesus will return any day, and all your work and suffering will be for nothing."

"If Jesus returns tomorrow," Bonhoeffer replied, "then tomorrow I'll rest from my labor. But today I have work to do. I must continue the struggle until it's finished."

Until Jesus returns for you and me, we have our lives to live and our work to do. There is no escape from the struggle of this life. As citizens of the kingdom of God we must have the integrity to admit this fact openly. Amid the joys and the laughter that is ours as children of the Author of all joys and pleasures, we must acknowledge that there will also be times of struggle. The important thing is that we are not alone in the fight.

The final and most important way we respond to the Christian struggle of Romans 7 is by allowing the Holy Spirit to aid us in our struggles. This is the crucial truth that ties Romans 7 and 8 together. Romans 7 presents the Christian struggle; Romans 8 introduces the Holy Spirit, who comes to aid us in our struggle.

We see how the Holy Spirit came to aid the early Christians in their struggle in Acts 4. The apostles Peter and John were brought before the Jewish authorities, threatened with death, warned not to preach anymore about Jesus, then released. Peter and John went back to their Christian friends and told how their lives had been threatened. Together, these Christians went before God in prayer, and this was their request: "Now, Lord, consider their threats and enable your servants to speak your word with great boldness" (Acts 4:29). Notice they did not pray that God would remove the threat or take them out of the struggle.

They didn't ask God for an easy road. They asked for boldness, for courage to continue the struggle.

In Acts 4:31 we see God's answer to their prayer: "After they prayed, the place where they were meeting was shaken. And they were all filled with the Holy Spirit and spoke the word of God boldly." The Holy Spirit didn't take them out of their struggle, but He came with power to aid them in their struggles.

The response of the believers in Acts must become our response as well. In prayer, acknowledging the reality of struggle in the Christian life, we invite the Holy Spirit to come and lead us through the struggle. That was the response of seventeen-year-old cancer patient, Cheryl Hall. Her story was told in a book called *Too Old to Cry . . . Too Young to Die*. She was going through a series of daily chemotherapy treatments that were almost unbearably painful. As she underwent treatment after treatment, she reflected, "I've learned that when they're going to do something more to you, you can't pray, 'God, don't let them hurt me.' You have to pray for the strength to cope with it."[1]

There is enormous wisdom and maturity in the words of this young woman of God. She is becoming conformed to the character and likeness of Jesus. For that, in fact, is the goal of the Christian life: Christlikeness. Part of the process of Christian maturity is coming to a place where, instead of praying, "God, take away this temptation, this struggle, this trial," we pray, "God, give me strength and courage to face this situation."

We are learning that if the Christian faith makes any sense at all, it *must* make sense amid the temptations, pressures, and sorrows of this broken world. If the Christian gospel doesn't make sense in the rough-and-tumble adventure of real life, it doesn't make sense, period. But thank God, it does make sense—especially as we allow the Holy Spirit to come and aid us in the good struggle of the Christian life.

Chapter 10

—— *All Things Work* ——
Together for **Whose** *Good?*
(Romans 8)

Dr. E. C. Caldwell, professor of New Testament at Union Theological Seminary in Richmond, Virginia, had just completed his lecture for the day. The subject of the class was the book of Romans. "Tomorrow," Dr. Caldwell concluded, "I will be teaching on the eighth chapter of Romans. So tonight, as you study this chapter, I want you to pay special attention to verse 28—'all things work together for good to them that love God.' As you study this verse in your Greek text, be careful to notice what this verse truly says—and what it doesn't say."

He paused, and looked around the room at the faces of the young seminarians. Then, sensing the prompting of the Holy Spirit, he added, "One final word before I dismiss you—Whatever happens in all the years to come, remember: Romans 8:28 will always hold true."

Later that day, Dr. Caldwell and his wife were driving in their car. They came to a railroad crossing, unaware that a freight train was swiftly bearing down on the crossing. The train plowed into their car, killing Mrs. Caldwell instantly. Severely injured, Dr. Caldwell was rushed by ambulance to a hospital, where doctors determined he would live, but would be left permanently handicapped.

Months later, Dr. Caldwell returned to the classroom. With the aid of a cane, he stood before the class. The room was hushed. The students, recalling that his last words to the class were, "Romans 8:28 will always hold true," awaited his first words since the tragedy. Dr. Caldwell looked into the face of each student. "Romans 8:28," he said. "It still holds true. One day we shall see God's good, even in this."

Romans 8:28 is one of the best loved yet least understood verses in the Bible. In this age of the "prosperity gospel" and "name-it-and-claim-it" theology, this verse has been treated as a kind of Christian good-luck charm. If a Christian loses a job or is injured in an accident or has suffered the death of a loved one, you can almost count on someone going to him or her and saying, "You just have to claim Romans 8:28. The reason you lost that job is because God wants to give you a better-paying job." Or, "Remember Romans 8:28. Something good is going to come out of this accident." Or, "Just trust in Romans 8:28. God called your loved one home for a good reason." In times of trial, this verse is often used (with the best of intentions) as an "answer" verse when people don't know what else to say.

During my own times of grief and trial—when my father died, when our newborn daughter was seriously ill, when my brother died of cancer—a number of well-meaning friends told me, "You just have to claim Romans 8:28 at a time like this." Though I was grateful for their caring, I have to say their counsel gave me no comfort or encouragement during those difficult times. So, from my own experience, I encourage you never to use this verse in such a way with your friends and loved ones.

I'm convinced that it does no good to glibly thrust Romans 8:28 at a person who is undergoing loneliness, depression, or grief. At best, your words will sound superficial and unfeeling. At worst, your words can even deepen that person's hurt, causing him or her to feel that all this hurt is really the result of not being spiritual enough, of not trusting enough in the promise of Romans 8:28. Worst of all, using this verse at such times distorts its meaning. What we are saying is that God is at work in every aspect of our lives to bring about *our* happiness, *our* prosperity, *our* success. That's not what this verse is about.

F. F. Bruce, in his commentary on Romans, reminds us of the apostle Paul's careful grammatical construction of this passage and points out that the subject of the sentence in Romans 8:28 is *God*. And if the subject of the sentence is *God*, then the word *good* must refer primarily to God's good, not yours or mine. This casts the truth of Romans 8:28 in an entirely different light. We see that the point of this verse is not that God is working to bring about our prosperity or momentary happiness, but to bring about *His* good, *His* eternal purpose.

Many of our contemporary Bible translations and paraphrases seem to miss this important distinction. The New International Version—an otherwise excellent and dependable study Bible—reads, "And we know that in all things God works *for the good of those who love him*, who have been called according to his purpose" (emphasis added). And The Living Bible—a Bible that has been very helpful in our family's daily devotional times—similarly misses what I believe to be the true thrust of this important verse when it says, "And we know that all that happens to us is working *for our good* if we love God and are fitting into his plans" (emphasis added).

The New English Bible offers an interesting slant on this verse: "And in everything, as we know, he co-operates for good with those who love God . . . ." Note the sense of cooperative partnership between us and God, a sense that we work together with God to further His plans. We catch a similar sense in the Revised Standard Version: "We know that in everything God works for good with those who love Him." Note the wording: God works for good, not *for* those who love Him, but *with* those who love Him.

When we approach a key biblical passage such as Romans 8:28, it's important that we take careful note of the subtle shading of meaning within that passage. We should examine its grammatical construction. We should place it in context with the surrounding Scripture. We should compare it with other passages to be sure that our interpretation of this verse does not conflict with the body of God's revealed Word. If we are careless in our handling of Scripture, we risk believing an illusion. And if we buy into an illusion about what the Bible teaches, we set ourselves up to be *dis*illusioned as our false conceptions run aground on the rocks of reality.

It's an illusion to view Romans 8:28 as a guarantee that all of life will turn out for our good—at least for what we human beings consider good: health, happiness, and prosperity. There are many events in life that are not good, and to pretend they are good is to deny our own feelings and to distort the truth of God's Word. There's nothing good about a financial loss, a broken marriage, an illness, or the death of a loved one. Yet these things happen. They happen even to those who love God and who have been called according to His purpose.

The good news is not that God will make our circumstances come out the way we like, but that God can weave even our disappointments and disasters into His eternal plan. The evil that happens to us can be transformed into God's good. Romans 8:28 is God's guarantee that if we love God, our lives can be used to achieve His purposes and further His kingdom. In our limited wisdom, this truth may not always feel good, it may not always make good sense by our reasoning—but by faith we can trust that God's promise is sure.

Let's look at the context of Romans 8:28. This verse is embedded in the flow of a very powerful chapter. The theme of this chapter is *the work of the Holy Spirit*. Paul opens chapter 8 by drawing a comparison between two different kinds of life—the life of the self (the ego or human nature) versus the life of the Spirit. This is a continuation of Paul's discussion of the Christian struggle that he begins in chapter 7. The solution to the struggle, says Paul, lies in being led by the Spirit rather than by the natural inclinations of sinful human nature.

The Greek word for *spirit* is *pneuma*, which is the same as the word for *breath*. Thus, Paul's discussion of the Holy Spirit in Romans 8 creates a dynamic image of our life in the Spirit. The Spirit is like the air we breathe. He surrounds us, we breathe Him into us, and He fills us and gives us life. When we are led by the Spirit and filled with the Spirit, we allow Him to fill our thoughts, our desires, and our will. We become Spirit-controlled people—and Romans 8:14 and 16 tells us that "those who are led [or controlled] by the Spirit of God are [children] of God . . . . The Spirit Himself testifies with our spirit that we are God's children."

Think of it! We are *children* of the living, eternal God of the Universe! And as Paul tells us in verse 17, our status as God's children means that we are also God's heirs and co-heirs with Jesus Christ. So if we share the sufferings of Christ, we will also share His glory. Paul points us toward the future glory that is ours as we live out our lives under the control of the Holy Spirit. He shows us the long view of history. "I consider that our present sufferings," he writes in Romans 8:18, "are not worth comparing with the glory that will be revealed in us."

Now, notice how Romans 8:18 links up with Romans 8:28 in a continuous, seamless thought: Paul says, in effect, "Yes! we will have suffering in this life—but those sufferings aren't even worth comparing to the glory to come! In fact, everything that happens to us, including our suffering, is woven into God's plan, which He is working out in our lives." Clearly, as we grasp the flow of Paul's argument, we are left with no excuse for viewing Romans 8:28 as a "good luck charm." Instead, we are forced to the realization that even our "bad luck" can be used to further God's kingdom.

C. S. Lewis once said that the most frequently spoken word in heaven would be, *Oh.* As in, "Oh, now I understand." Or, "Oh, now I see what God's plan was." Or, "Oh, now I see the reason for the trial I went through." In eternity, we will at last have the long view of history. We will have the answers to our questions. We will have 20/20 hindsight stretching back to the beginning of time, and we will understand.

The problem you and I have is that, for now, we have to get along with a very limited perspective. We see, as Paul observed in 1 Corinthians 13, as though we are looking in a dark mirror. Our understanding is like a dim reflection. But thanks to Romans 8:28, we have the certainty that if we love God, we will one day look back—if not in this life, then at least in eternity—and we will know that all things woven together have worked out for God's good. God has been able to use our weak and limited resources to create something enduring, something eternal. His glory has been revealed in you and me.

In verse 29, we discover one important part of God's eternal purpose—and what a tremendous affirmation this is for your life and mine! Paul writes, "For those God foreknew He also predestined to be conformed to the likeness of His Son, that he might be the firstborn among many brothers." Here Paul tells us God has made a decision ahead of time about you and me, about every person who truly loves Jesus Christ. God has decided to use all the circumstances of our lives to accomplish a grand purpose in our lives—and that purpose is that you and I would become conformed to the image and character of His Son, Jesus Christ.

Now we begin to see why Romans 8:28 should never be yanked out of its context. Verses 28 and 29 form a single continuous thought and should always be linked together. A good paraphrase of these verses might be, "We know that God weaves all circumstances into His good plan in partnership with those who love Him, who have been called according to His purpose; for God in His foreknowledge has made a decision ahead of time that they might be shaped into the image, the likeness, the character of His Son Jesus, so that Jesus might be the firstborn Son of God, and we might be Jesus' brothers and sisters as children of God."

What an exalted position we hold in the kingdom of God! Do you begin to get a glimpse of the eternal scope of God's plan, and how you and I—along with all our circumstances, our joys, our hurts—are woven into that plan? Do you see the great adventure God has reserved for you, an adventure of growing more and more like Jesus Christ? And do you begin to see how God is able to use even evil experiences to shape us, to make us more mature, more Christlike?

As president of the Fellowship of Christian Athletes, James Jeffries was one of the most articulate and dynamic Christian spokesmen in the country. In many ways, Jeffries' son Neil was a lot like his dad—strongly built, athletic, good looking, and with a deep commitment to Jesus Christ. In fact, Neil was such an outstanding athlete that he was awarded a football scholarship to Baylor University, where as quarterback he led Baylor to its first conference championship in fifty years.

But there was one respect in which Neil Jeffries was as different from his father, James Jeffries, as night and day. For while James was a dynamic and charismatic public speaker, Neil was afflicted with a severe stutter. I came to know Neil when we were in an FCA Bible study some years ago, and I saw in him a shy but thoughtful, wise, intelligent young man. I thought it a tragedy that so much of this fine young man's personality and thinking should be trapped behind a wall of stammering.

Sometime later, I was surprised to see that Neil had been chosen to speak at an FCA national conference.

Over a thousand young athletes were in attendance as Neil stepped onto the platform and began to speak. Many in the audience didn't know about Neil's speech impediment, and some, thinking his performance was a joke or a skit, began to laugh.

On the platform, however, Neil continued talking. It took him about twenty minutes to say what you or I could have said in five or ten minutes. There was nothing eloquent or charismatic about his speech. Yet at the conclusion of Neil's talk, something amazing happened. Neil offered an invitation for those in the audience to give their lives to Jesus Christ. All across the audience, young men stood and began to walk forward. One FCA staffer commented that more young athletes made a commitment of their lives to Christ at that moment than at any other FCA conference. God accomplished something through Neil's brokenness that could never have been achieved through strength.

For me, that was a powerful proof of the truth of Romans 8:28 and 29. God was weaving Neil's brokenness into His eternal plan, calling young lives into His kingdom while shaping Neil's character to become more like Christ's. Neil's speech impediment was not a good thing, but God was able to use Neil as His partner in furthering the kingdom.

Neil's testimony demonstrates an important principle of evangelism: We should never "bait" others into receiving Christ with the false promise that their lives will become easier as a result. Carried to its logical conclusion, a "gospel" that preaches that Christ has come to make our lives easier is actually a "gospel" of selfishness. God's purpose in this universe is far greater than merely putting an extra car in our garage or a big-screen TV in our living room. Certainly, God cares about our happiness, but God's Word clearly teaches that our ultimate happiness is found in God Himself, not in possessions or circumstances.

In an average month, I come in contact with scores of people in tragic circumstances: a couple whose son has just told them he is living an unrepentant homosexual lifestyle; a husband whose chronically depressed wife has just attempted suicide for the fourth time; a mother whose only son has died in an accident at the age of ten; a Christian man in his sixties who has lost his savings and his career in a business failure; a mother in her thirties who has just been diagnosed with terminal cancer. You don't go to such a person and say, "Just claim Romans 8:28." There's nothing good in these tragedies. In time, God may enable such a person to gain a clearer perspective on his or her trial. But to quote Romans 8:28 out of context during such times constitutes insensitivity to that person's feelings and to the Spirit of God.

What does the Bible counsel us to do for our hurting friends? Galatians 6:2 says, "Carry each other's burdens, and in this way you will fulfill the law of Christ." Look carefully at those words: *the law of Christ.* This is not a "suggestion" of Christ; this is a command.

How do we carry each other's burdens? Not by glibly reciting Bible verses. We carry our Christian brothers' and sisters' burdens when we pray with them, when we embrace them, when we love them and listen to them. Our presence is often the most helpful when we offer no advice, when we are simply available to our hurting friends as good listeners. Unfortunately, many people are reluctant to be open about their burdens because the last time they had a problem they received only a spiritual pat on the back, a verse of Scripture, and a swift good-bye.

We will never fulfill the command of Christ until we are willing to get in the trenches beside our Christian brothers and sisters. We cannot authentically claim to love others unless we place our shoulders next to theirs and strain beneath their burdens with them. We must love in a deep and costly way. We must take the hurt of our brothers and sisters into our own souls, mingling our tears with theirs.

Are you that kind of friend to others? Don't you want to be surrounded by such friends when tears, burdens, and hurts come into your own life? For the message of Romans 8 is that such trials lie ahead for all of us.

If we have the integrity to interpret verse 28 within the flow of the entire eighth chapter of Romans, we are forced to acknowledge that God has not called us to a life of ease and bliss. The verses that follow verse 28 deal with some very harsh circumstances indeed, with trials such as "trouble or hardship or persecution or famine or nakedness or danger or sword" (v. 35). Yet the message of Paul is that in all these things, even in death itself, we are more than conquerors through Him who loves us:

> For I am convinced that neither death nor life, neither angels nor demons, neither the present nor the future, nor any powers, neither height nor depth, nor anything else in all creation, will be able to separate us from the love of God that is in Christ Jesus our Lord (Romans 8:38–39).

In other words, Paul is telling us that the future is uncertain, there are perils all around us, the grave lies at the end of our journey—yet none of these things can separate us from God's infinite love. Through Him, we are more than conquerors, regardless of our circumstances. As Fritz Ridenour writes in his popular commentary on these verses, "For the Christian, every cloud doesn't have a silver lining, but behind the clouds the sun is always shining."[1]

As we examine Romans 8:28 in the flow of its context, it gives us an *eternal* context for our lives, our hurts, and our faith. Through the lens of Romans 8 we can see how God is able to use even the worst that life can throw at us to make us more mature and Christlike, and to further the purposes of His kingdom. When we understand that God's primary concern is our Christlikeness—not our happiness, success, health, and prosperity—then we are able to honestly face this all-important question:

Do you love God enough to say, "Lord, I want you to use me any way you can to advance your plan?" That's a tough question. But ultimately, it's the most crucial question we face in this life.

The missionary pioneer William Carey didn't consider it a good thing when God called him away from the comfort of home and family to labor and die for Jesus Christ in India. Armando Valladares didn't consider it a good thing to be confined in a Cuban prison for twenty-two years, subject to indescribable tortures, forced to march through ditches of raw sewage, and fed on food tainted with kerosene. Joni Eareckson Tada didn't consider it a good thing to awake after a diving accident and find herself paralyzed from the neck down, forced to spend the rest of her life in a wheelchair. It would take time—years, and even decades of time—for William Carey and Armando Valladares and Joni Eareckson Tada to see the impact that their suffering and sacrifice would have on many thousands of lives.

In this life, you and I may never see our own pain woven in God's eternal plan. We may not catch a glimpse of the meaning of our suffering until eternity. But in Romans 8 we have God's certain promise that one day we shall look back and say, "Oh, now I understand. Now I see, Lord, you knew what you were doing all along."

Chapter 11

Old Faith for a New Age
(Romans 9–11)

"Ron," said the pastor of the church, "I'm Rev. Wilson. We have a few minutes before the service begins. Would you come into my study for a moment?"

I accompanied Rev. Wilson into his study, thinking he wanted to spend a few minutes in prayer before the worship service. I was wrong. "Tell me, Ron," he said, closing the door behind him, "what are your laypeople going to say to my congregation?"

I was in my twenties at the time, fresh out of seminary, and I was part of a lay witness mission team visiting Rev. Wilson's church. We had traveled from our church in Minneapolis to a church in northern Minnesota. The idea behind the lay witness mission program was to give laypeople a chance to speak publicly in other churches about what God had done in their lives. "Well," I replied, "each person in our group will share about his or her own relationship with Jesus Christ."

"Of course," replied Rev. Wilson, impatiently brushing aside my reply. "That's what they'll be talking about *generally*. I want to know *specifically* what they'll be saying. I trust you went over each person's talk in detail before you came here."

"No, I didn't. I didn't think it was necessary."

He seemed shocked, even alarmed. "You didn't?!—"

"I just told them to get up on the platform and share from their hearts how Jesus had changed their lives, their families, their relationships with others."

Rev. Wilson began to wring his hands and stammer, "But—but these laypeople—I mean, what sort of theological training do they have? After all, without the right sort of religious instruction they might get up there and say just about *anything!*"

Rev. Wilson's fears were unjustified. During the service, each of my friends got up and simply shared from his or her own heart. The members of Rev. Wilson's congregation were challenged and encouraged to hear what God was doing in the lives of other laypeople just like themselves.

Unfortunately, there are many people—pastors and laypeople alike—who think like Rev. Wilson, who see the task of telling other people about Jesus Christ as a job for people with "theological training." All too many Christians excuse themselves from the task of evangelism by saying, "Oh, I don't have the sort of training to witness to other people. I don't know the Bible well enough. What if someone asks me a question I can't answer? What if I make a fool of myself?"

How tragic! When He founded His Church two thousand years ago, Jesus didn't intend to build a wall between "professional" and "lay" Christians. He gave His Great Commission to "go and make disciples" to *all* Christians, in every culture, at every educational level, at every economic level, in all ages of history.

A number of years ago, I heard Dr. Robert Munger, former professor at Fuller Theological Seminary, give a talk on lay ministry. There was one statement he made that has stuck with me ever since.

Christianity, in its beginning, was a lay movement. Later on the early church would be joined by a number of priests and a few highly trained, educated professionals such as Stephen and the apostle Paul. But they were the exception, and not the rule. For the most part, the ministry and missionary activity of the early church were carried out by non-professionals, ordinary men and women involved in secular work.

It's not the job of pastors, teachers, and missionaries to carry the entire burden of evangelizing the world. In Ephesians 4:11–13, we find that the role of so-called "professional" Christians is to encourage, train, and equip "lay" Christians to carry out the work of the church, including the work of evangelism. Not every Christian is called to preach to thousands like Billy Graham or Luis Palau, but every Christian is called to be a witness to others of what God has done in his or her own life.

As we come to Romans 9 to 11, we find that the task of evangelism was very much on the mind of the apostle Paul. In the first few verses of Romans 9, he pours out a heart filled with love, sorrow, and urgency toward those lost without Jesus Christ. He writes:

I speak the truth in Christ—I am not lying, my conscience confirms it in the Holy Spirit—I have great sorrow and unceasing anguish in my heart. For I could wish that I myself were cursed and cut off from Christ for the sake of my brothers, those of my own race, the people of Israel . . . . Brothers, my heart's desire and prayer

to God for the Israelites is that they may be
saved (Romans 9:1–4; 10:1).

Here, Paul agonizes over his own Jewish kinfolk, many
of whom have rejected his message of salvation through
faith in Christ. Whether through ignorance or willful
disobedience, many of Paul's countrymen have decided
to place their trust not in Christ but in their own
genealogy as descendants of Abraham. So wounded and
grieved is Paul that he actually wishes he could be
eternally damned in the place of his fellow Jews if he
could win their salvation.

I read these passionate words of Paul and I think to
myself, "What a heart for human souls this man had!
What a heart for sharing Christ with others! What love
for people he had!" And I have to wonder: *Do I have
this kind of love for people*? Could I honestly say I
would willingly cut myself off from Christ (if that were
possible) so that others could know Him? I have to
confess that, in light of Romans 9, my own love seems
so shallow. Yet I *want* to have that kind of love for
others. It is this kind of passionate caring for people
that motivates us to reach out and love others into the
kingdom of God.

In terms of the structure of Romans, chapters 9, 10,
and 11 form a kind of parenthesis or interlude in the
middle of Paul's argument. To the modern reader, the
message of these chapters sometimes gets lost amid all
of Paul's allusions to Old Testament people and events.
Yet on closer examination, we find some very striking
parallels between Paul's age and our own.

The people of Paul's beloved Israel have become
spiritually complacent, self-sufficient, and self-righteous—
and thus they have become very difficult to reach with the

gospel of Jesus Christ. For centuries, Israel has regarded itself as God's chosen nation, a society blessed above all others purely on the basis of Israel's descent from Abraham. Since Old Testament times, Israel has enjoyed a special covenant relationship with God. It was to Israel that the Law of Moses was given. The people of Israel had a sense of promise, tradition, and destiny rooted in their historic relationship with God.

Paul, who had been suddenly converted to faith in Christ after a dramatic experience on the Damascus road, fully understood the pride of Israel. He himself had been a proud, Pharisaic Jew, a persecutor of the Christian church. It took a dazzling miracle of God's power to break down Paul's pride and pierce his heart. So Paul identified completely with the stubborn resistance of Israel to the Christian gospel.

In this passage, the heart of Paul is completely transparent. Even though he has endured intense persecution, stoning, beatings, riots, and bitter accusations from his Jewish countrymen, he does not see himself as their enemy. He loves them and hurts over them. His own desire is to win his people over to a saving faith in Jesus Christ. He wants them to know that God's acceptance does not depend on being biologically descended from Abraham. Nor, as he says in Romans 9:16, does salvation "depend on man's desire or effort." Salvation is purely a matter of trusting in the grace of God and the sacrifice of Jesus Christ.

Quoting the promises God gave through Moses, Hosea, and Isaiah, Paul seeks to penetrate the spiritual and racial pride of his Jewish listeners. He is attempting to demonstrate from the Hebrew Scriptures themselves that the gospel of wholeness he sets forth in Romans is not the invention of some bizarre religious cult, but rather a consistent extension of all that God has been doing since the world began.

Though Paul's message in this section is addressed to the particular problem of the Jewish rejection of Christ, this message has a powerful application in our own culture of the 1990s. The people we work with, go to school with, meet in line at the checkout stand, and rub shoulders with at the shopping mall are essentially no different from the proud Jews of Paul's day.

Many of those we come in contact with are complacent, feeling God will accept them because they are "good" people who try to live "good" lives. Others place their trust in Eastern religion, "religious science" meditation techniques, or the psycho-babble of the latest "New Age" guru. Others have a bland belief that "all roads lead to God." Many are simply indifferent to spiritual things because they are caught up in the idolatry of self-fulfillment, success, and the pursuit of wealth and power. Still others are simply hostile toward Jesus Christ.

With this as our perspective, Paul's message in Romans 9 to 11 begins to have a familiar ring, doesn't it? Then, as now, the problem of evangelism is, how do we penetrate the spiritual complacency, pride, and self-righteousness of our age so that we can share what Jesus Christ has done in our lives? In Romans, Paul presents us with an old faith for a "New Age." We have a faith that is reliable and relevant, despite the dizzying maelstrom of cults, philosophies, and "isms" that swirl about us.

In chapter 10, Paul explains the plan of salvation by faith in Jesus Christ. In a passage sprinkled with quotations from the Old Testament writings of Isaiah, Moses, Joel, and the Psalms, he writes:

> . . . if you confess with your mouth, "Jesus is
> Lord," and believe in your heart that God raised
> him from the dead, you will be saved. For it is
> with your heart that you believe and are
> justified, and it is with your mouth that you
> confess and are saved. As the Scripture says,
> "Anyone who trusts in him will never be put to
> shame." For there is no difference between Jew
> and Gentile—the same Lord is Lord of all and
> richly blesses all who call on him, for,
> "Everyone who calls on the name of the Lord
> will be saved" (Romans 10:9–13).

That's our gospel in a nutshell. Paul goes on to
confront us with our responsibility to share that gospel
with those around us:

> How, then, can they call on the one they have
> not believed in? And how can they believe in
> the one of whom they have not heard? And how
> can they hear without someone preaching to
> them? And how can they preach unless they are
> sent? As it is written, "How beautiful are the
> feet of those who bring good news!" (Romans
> 10:14–15).

Now, don't let that word "preach" throw you. Paul is
simply telling us that the people around us, the people
we come in contact with every day, cannot believe in
Jesus Christ, if no one bothers to *tell* them about Jesus
Christ. That's your job and mine.

And what does Paul mean when he writes, "How can
they preach unless they are sent?" Ray Stedman, in his
commentary on Romans, *From Guilt to Glory*, replies,
"There need be no doubt as to the One who does the
sending. Jesus Himself said, 'Pray the Lord of the

harvest, that He may send forth laborers.' It is God who sends [men and women]."[1] The Lord of the harvest is calling on you and me to take the gospel of wholeness to people around us, people broken by sin.

We have a message of good news, the best news this tired old world has ever heard. That's why Paul writes, quoting Isaiah 52:7, "How beautiful are the feet of those who bring good news!" Now, most people would agree that feet are not what we usually think of as the most "beautiful" parts of the body. Yet, as Paul tells us in this passage, even that which is humble and unlovely becomes a thing of beauty when it brings the good news of God's saving grace. So it is with you and me.

We may not see ourselves as attractive, eloquent, filled with Bible knowledge, or possessed of a winsome personality. We may even see ourselves as mere humble "feet" in the body of Christ. But as we lovingly and obediently take the good news we have received from God and share it with those around us, we become beautiful in the eyes of God—and in the eyes of those whose lives are affected by our witness.

Ron Jensen, President of the International Graduate School of Theology, tells about an experience he had when he was in his early twenties. He had just undergone a course in evangelism. In this course, he had learned that an effective way to witness is by building a relationship of trust and credibility with a non-Christian. After taking this training, Ron believed he had discovered the "right" way to witness.

One day, Ron was in a big crowd on a Seattle street, watching a parade. Among the people thronging the parade route, he noticed one shabbily dressed young man. This fellow was stopping people in the street and handing each one a Christian tract. Ron took this young man aside and said, "Excuse me, I appreciate the fact that you're a Christian and you want to share your faith with other people. But don't you know that you shouldn't witness to people by simply shoving a tract in their hands? Don't you realize that the best way to share Christ is by building a relationship with them first?"

The young man looked a little hurt—and then he began to stammer. "I . . . I-I-I love . . . J-j-j-j-jee . . . s-s-sus," he began. And in this tortured stammer, he explained to Ron Jensen that he loved Jesus, but was unable to communicate with others effectively. The only way he knew to share the love of Jesus with other people was by handing out tracts.

Ron Jensen concludes that he learned an enormous lesson that day. There is no one "right" way to witness. There is only a gospel, and those who share it in the way that is the most natural and effective for them. No matter how we share the good news of Jesus Christ, the truth of Romans 10:15 and of Isaiah 52:7 applies: "How beautiful are the feet of those who bring good news!" The young man with his tracts on that Seattle street may have had shabby clothes and inelegant speech, but his heart and his "feet" were beautiful.

The crucial questions confronting you and me from Romans 9 through 11 are these: Are your feet "beautiful" today? Are the people around you, the people you come in contact with every day, closer to an eternity with Jesus Christ because of your influence? Or do you just pass among them like a vague fog, your Christianity unfelt and unseen, having no affect on their eternal destinies?

There are many ways to share your faith with the people around you. Not everyone is either comfortable or most effective handing out tracts on a street corner, but all of us have friends with whom we can simply be ourselves over a cup of coffee. Our relationship with Jesus Christ should be the most important part of who we are, a part of ourselves that we naturally want to share with others. If you need more encouragement or insight into how to share your faith with your friends, neighbors, and associates, check your Christian bookstore or church library for such books as *Life-Style Evangelism: Crossing Traditional Boundaries to Reach the Unbelieving World* by Joseph C. Aldrich (Multnomah, 1981) and *Out of the Saltshaker & Into the World: Evangelism As a Way of Life* by Rebecca Manley Pippert (InterVarsity, 1979).

There are two things we should keep in mind whenever we share our faith with others. First, we should remember that *we are not sharing a religion; we are sharing a relationship*. Throughout Romans 9, 10, and 11, we see Paul drawing a vivid contrast: the *religion* of his Jewish kinspeople versus the *relationship* between a Christian and his Lord Jesus Christ. Religion puts an emphasis on structure; relationship emphasizes the Savior. Religion says, "Become part of a system"; relationship says, "Get to know a Person." Religion says, "Work hard and gain God's favor"; relationship says, "Receive Christ and accept God's grace." Religion says, "Reach up to God"; the relationship of the Christian faith says, "God has reached out to us through the cross of Jesus Christ."

Our gospel is not a collection of rules to live by. Our gospel is not a denomination. Our gospel is not a body of doctrines. Our gospel is a *Person*. When we share Christ, we are not merely trying to convince the non-

Christian that we are right. We are truly introducing that non-Christian to a Friend.

Second thing we should remember when sharing Christ: *Our motivation for witnessing to others is not a sense of obligation.* It is not a desire to rack up converts like points in a game. Our motivation for witnessing is not to increase church membership or to feel good about ourselves. Our motivation for witnessing must be a genuine love for people. Our motivation should be a reflection of the love Paul expresses when he writes, "For I could wish that I myself were cursed and cut off from Christ for the sake of my brothers . . . . My heart's desire and prayer to God . . . is that they may be saved." Nothing less than a heart of love is a pure motivation for evangelism.

Some years ago, I was talking with Keith Phillips, founder and president of World Impact, a compassionate and evangelistic ministry to American inner cities. Keith told me the story of a little boy named Michael who was growing up in the streets of a barrio in southern California. The reason Michael was on the streets was that his mother locked him out of the apartment every morning. She never gave him breakfast, and rarely troubled herself to fix him dinner. She had a boyfriend who spent the day and most of the evening at her apartment, and neither she nor her boyfriend wanted a little boy around to bother them.

As soon as Michael was shoved out the door in the morning, he would set about the task of scrounging a morning meal. He would start by picking through the garbage bins in the alley behind the liquor store, often finding stale peanuts and pretzels to eat. Then he would hit the street and panhandle until he had enough change for a Snickers bar from the gas station vending machine.

Some days, Michael couldn't find anything to eat in the garbage bins, and he couldn't beg the price of a Snickers bar. So he would go to the World Impact house a few blocks away, because he knew that the Christian people there were compassionate, and he could always count on a square meal there.

Keith Phillips always made a point of being a friend to Michael whenever he came by the World Impact house. One day, Keith was walking past an alley and saw Michael scrounging in the garbage bin. He followed Michael to the street and watched him beg for coins. Finally, he stepped up and put his hand on the boy's shoulder. Michael turned, startled.

"Michael," Keith said, bending down to look the boy in the eye. "I didn't know you were living like this. Why don't you just come over to the World Impact house and get a good meal every morning?"

"Mr. Keith, my mother doesn't love me. Nobody else loves me. You Christians are the only ones who love me, so I never want to take advantage of you."

Michael knew genuine Christian love when he found it. This Christlike love for others is our reason for witnessing. We see this kind of love reflected in the heart of Paul, at the core of the book of Romans. Our prayer should be that others would find God's love reflected in you and me as we proclaim our enduring faith in this changing age of the 1990s.

Chapter 12

— *The Christian* —
Non-Conformist
(Romans 12:1–2)

Early one morning in the middle 1800s, a young man named William Booth climbed a hillside overlooking the city of London. He knelt in the grass, spread his Bible open, and prayed, "Father, I know there are men with greater courage than William Booth. And I know there are men with greater intellect than William Booth. And I know there are men with greater ability than William Booth. But Father, I promise you this day that you shall have *all* the courage and *all* the intellect and *all* the abilities of William Booth. You shall have all there is of William Booth."

Booth went down from that hillside and stepped into the grimy streets of London, a transformed man with a renewed mind. Over the years that followed, Booth ministered to the needs of thousands of physically and spiritually broken men and women of London. His ministry grew and spread to encompass all of England, and then all of Europe. It spread to America, and then around the globe.

Today, the ministry William Booth founded in 1864 continues to meet the spiritual and physical needs of broken men and women around the world. That ministry—The Salvation Army—still takes the gospel of wholeness to a broken world because one young man made a decision to offer his life as a living sacrifice to God.

In Romans 12:1–2 Paul writes:

> Therefore, I urge you, brothers, in view of God's mercy, to offer your bodies as living sacrifices, holy and pleasing to God—this is your spiritual act of worship. Do not conform any longer to the pattern of this world, but be transformed by the renewing of your mind. Then you will be able to test and approve what God's will is—his good, pleasing and perfect will.

Here, at the beginning of Romans 12, Paul contrasts the Christian world view against the world view of this present age. Paul's counsel in verse 2, "Do not conform any longer to the pattern of this world," might be translated, "Do not let the world squeeze you into its mold," or, "Challenge the right of this present age to set the agenda for your life."

So we must take a hard look at the world view of the age in which we live, contrasting it with the world view we find in the Word of God. The problem many of us have as Christians in the 1990s is that we have been profoundly influenced by philosophies, ideas, and values that are explicitly non-Christian—yet we are completely unaware this influence has taken place. We don't even realize how greatly the thought forms of this broken world have shaped the agenda for our lives.

I think, for example, of the many college students who have come into my counseling room, saying, "Ron, I'm going to take a year off and hitchhike across America, or travel across Europe, or live on the beach. I just have to take some time off to find myself." These young people seem to feel that if they could just peel away all the socially prescribed layers that their parents, their church, their school, and their society have imposed on them, they would discover a pure, liberated, pre-existent self.

One of the basic assumptions of our age is that the only way to find meaning and purpose in life is to "find" ourselves, to "get in touch" with our inner selves. The problem with this world view is that once we have peeled away all those layers of the onion, we are likely to find *nothing* at the center. That, ultimately, is where the narcissistic self-fulfillment movements of the 1970s and '80s have led us. The result has not only been despair and disillusionment but increased suffering in the world.

Young people remain single longer these days than the previous generation—not merely because they view the institution of marriage as a failure (which it often is), but because they see marriage as restrictive. They think, "If I marry, my spouse is only going to limit me, thwart my ambition, inhibit my self-expression. I refuse to allow anything or anyone to limit me in any way."

The mood of our times was powerfully expressed some years ago in the film *Kramer vs. Kramer*. Here's the scenario: Joanne Kramer (played by Meryl Streep) walks out on her husband, Ted, and their six-year-old son because she needs to "find" herself. Shortly afterwards, a neighbor—who is a close friend of Joanne's—comes by to offer consolation to Ted Kramer (Dustin Hoffman), remarking, "You may not realize it today, Ted, but what Joanne has done is really a courageous thing." Ted's reply: "Really? How courageous is it to walk out on your six-year-old son?"

The view that we should assert our selfish demands and reject responsibility has become a social norm in our society as we continue our headlong plunge in pursuit of self. What we are seeing is a fulfillment of our Lord's prediction that, "because of the increase of wickedness, the love of most will grow cold" (Matthew 24:12). This mad stampede of rampant selfishness leaves in its wake the bruised and trampled souls of children—children like Ted and Joanne Kramer's little boy, and even children who never get a chance to be born.

Every year, 1.6 million babies are aborted. Fewer than two percent of these abortions are performed for medically therapeutic reasons (that is, involving a threat to the health of the mother) or for rape or incest.[1] More than ninety-eight percent of all abortions are a result of a woman's decision that a baby would interfere with her lifestyle or restrict her options in life. In other words, nearly all abortions today are the result of a woman saying, "I'm not willing to take this responsibility."

Some time ago, a *New York Times* article carried the headline "SEX-BASED ABORTION TREND NOW COMMON." It reported that the routine practice of amniocentesis (a medical test that can determine, among other things, the sex of a fetus) has resulted in increasing numbers of abortions because the baby was found to be the "wrong" sex. It is no longer unusual for a couple to say, "We already have a little girl. We just want to keep trying until we get a boy." It has even been reported that women have obtained abortions because a pregnancy would interfere with vacation plans, or would force a couple to put off buying a car or appliance. The word "choice" has become a polite code-word for *selfishness*.

In his book *Love and Will*, Rollo May describes what he calls "the new puritanism." Under the *old* puritanism, a young woman was made to feel guilty if she engaged in illicit sexual relationships. Under the *new* puritanism, she is made to feel guilty if she is *not* sexually active. Moreover, our society is conditioning young women to believe that the only responsible choice to make if they become pregnant is abortion. Motherhood or adoption are treated with contempt in much of the propaganda aimed at young women. Despite all the talk of "choice," many women with problem pregnancies are made to feel they really have *no* choice at all.

Our society has lost its moral compass and its compassion. The cohesion our civilization once enjoyed—a cohesion built around a framework of Judeo-Christian values—has seriously deteriorated. The lesson of history is that whenever a society cuts itself adrift from moral and ethical absolutes, that society has begun its slide toward chaos.

Having drawn this bleak picture of the world view of our age, we can better understand what Paul means when he says, in effect, "Don't conform any longer to the pattern of this world. Don't let the world squeeze you into its mold. Challenge the right of this present age to set the agenda for your life." The biblical Christian must live in contrast to the surrounding culture, continually on guard against the dead philosophies and values of this broken world, which seek to infiltrate our thinking.

Unfortunately, many Christians have not taken the time to find out for themselves what the world view of God's Word really is. Some Christians think the phrase "Know thyself" comes from the Bible. But it was Socrates, not Jesus, who said, "Know thyself" and it is an expression of Greek humanist philosophy, not Christianity. The philosophy of Jesus Christ is not "Know thyself," but "Know thy Creator." When you know your Creator, as revealed through Jesus Christ, then you will experience an identity, a sense of self-worth, a sense of fulfillment, meaning, and purpose that can never be found in the values and systems of this broken world.

Though there is value in the healthy introspection that goes along with prayer, meditation, and Christian counseling, our society has taken introspection to extremes of self-absorption and self-worship. Jesus directly confronts the narcissistic values of our time, saying, "Whoever finds his life will lose it, and whoever loses his life for my sake will find it." So significant is this statement that it's the only quotation of Christ recorded in all four gospels,[2] and it parallels Paul's counsel to "offer your bodies as living sacrifices, holy and pleasing to God."

Doesn't the word "sacrifice" sound strange and out-of-place in this era of selfishness? Clearly, this is not an age that places a great premium on personal sacrifice.

Years ago, when I was the Bible teacher for the Minnesota Vikings, I met a player who was one of the most famous names in professional football. In those days, he was very active in the Christian faith and an avid student of the Bible. Today, he has drifted far from the faith he once embraced. He has allowed the world to squeeze him into its mold.

Not long ago, a friend of mine had a long talk with this ex-Viking. The two of them, now both in their forties and living very different lives than when they had last seen each other, discussed all the changes they had undergone in the past few years. Toward the end of their talk, my friend asked, "What do you really think life is all about?"

The ex-football star replied, "I've come to believe that what life is really all about is accumulation."

Accumulation. We live in an age that teaches that fulfillment comes from accumulating the symbols and idols of that ultimate pagan god, Affluence. As we contrast these values with the message of sacrifice in Romans 12:1–2, a question occurs: How do we preach a gospel of sacrifice in a time when the *last* thing anyone wants to do is sacrifice?

I believe there is only one answer: We do not compromise. We do not equivocate. We meet the issue head-on. We state clearly that the self-centered mood of our culture is a fraud, a false promise. The person who is committed to the fulfillment of self is doomed to *emptiness* of self. The only way to authentic fulfillment is through self-sacrifice, through commitment to a cause and a Person *greater* than ourselves.

Many quarters of the Christian church preach a gospel of accommodation with our broken world, a gospel that says, in effect, "Go ahead and seek the fulfillment of the self. Accumulate wealth, accumulate symbols of status and achievement, accumulate glory for yourself—just as long as you think nice religious thoughts along the way."

A pastor in one prominent American church has said, "The two great things we need to learn in the church are, first, better showmanship and, second, how to give the people what they want." No! The Sermon on the Mount was a message of confrontation. It grated on the ears of first-century culture, and it grates on our ears as well.

The Christian gospel offers comfort for the afflicted, but it also afflicts the comfortable. It's a call to sacrifice.

I agree with Chuck Colson, who said, "The greatest heresy that confronts the church these days is the 'what's in it for me' gospel." The message of Romans 12:1-2 is not, "Water down your gospel until it is palatable to the rest of the world," but, "Do not let the world squeeze you into its mold!" Our task is not to accommodate to the dead values of our culture, but to confront them. We must state clearly that a devotion to selfish accumulation is a retreat from maturity, a retreat into self-delusion.

Of course, when we say such things, the world will protest, "But that sounds restrictive!" Our reply: "If that sounds restrictive, it's because it *is* restrictive." The gospel of wholeness in Romans 12:1-2 is a gospel of *slavery*, a glorious slavery in which we yield our whole selves to God and live our lives under His lordship. Jesus Christ must become not merely our Friend, not merely our Savior, but the *Lord* over every dimension of our lives.

After calling us to present ourselves as a living sacrifice, Paul adds an interesting clause that the New International Version renders, "which is your spiritual worship." The King James Version of that clause reads, "which is your reasonable service." The New American Standard Bible reads, "which is your spiritual service of worship," and adds a margin note that suggests that the word "rational" might be substituted for "spiritual." What is Paul saying here?

I suspect Paul deliberately chose a word with a double-edged meaning, suggesting that when we lay down our lives as living sacrifices to God, we are *both* performing an act of spiritual worship *and* we are doing only what is reasonable in return to God for all He has done for us. There are other Greek words Paul could have used that unambiguously mean "spiritual" or that unambiguously mean "reasonable." He might have used the Greek word *pneumatikos*, as he did in Romans 1:11, when he spoke about "spiritual" gifts, or in Romans 7:14, where he said "the law is spiritual." He might have used the Greek word *arestos*, as the disciples did in Acts 6:2, when they said it is not "reasonable" or "fitting" for minor matters to impede the proclamation of the gospel.

But in Romans 12:1, Paul selected the Greek word *logikos*, from which we get our English word "logic." Literally it refers to something that proceeds "from the word." Paul is saying that when we present ourselves as living sacrifices to God, this is only logical and reasonable—*and* it's the only response that conforms to the Word of God. All other attempts to worship God, short of sacrificially placing our very lives on the altar, are simply not enough. Religiousness and churchianity are not authentic spiritual worship. They are not even logical activities in view of the *infinite* sacrifice God made for us in offering Jesus on the cross. Thus, Romans 12:1 parallels Paul's counsel in 1 Corinthians 6:19–20: "You are not your own; you were bought at a price. Therefore honor God with your body."

Early in our marriage, Shirley and I owned a 1965 Chevy. With over 100,000 miles on the odometer, it had been driven through many harsh Minnesota winters—and it looked like it. Among our friends, this battered old Chevy was affectionately known as "The Rustmobile." We eventually sold it to a friend for $100. After closing the deal, Shirley and I came home and found an extra Rustmobile key in a drawer. The next day, I took the key to the new owner and said, "I forgot to give you this key yesterday." End of story.

But what if, instead of giving him that key, I used it to open the car and turn on the ignition? What if I had started backing the Rustmobile down my friend's driveway and out into the street? The new owner would have come charging out his front door, shouting, "What are you doing with my car?!"

I might answer, "Oh, I just thought I'd start 'er up and run some errands. You see, I still have this key and—"

"Wait a minute, Ron," he would reply. "Yesterday, I bought that car from you. It was bought at a price. It belongs to me now."

"Sure, I remember, but we've invested a lot of miles in this car. It's kind of hard to give it up, just like that."

And my friend would reach into his pocket and pull out the pink slip I had signed over to him the day before. "See this piece of paper, Ron? It means the car you're sitting in is mine. *All* mine. Not one of its rusty nuts or bolts belongs to you anymore. Even that key in the ignition belongs to me. So get out of the driver's seat. *Now.*"

He would have every right to say that to me. He's the new owner. In the same way, God is the new owner, the rightful owner, of your life and mine. Yet we resist His demand on our lives. We resist the restrictions He places on us. And that's the problem with a *living* sacrifice: It keeps crawling off the altar.

But God has a right to demand our sacrifice. Sacrificial living is only our reasonable, logical service, for we have been bought at a price.

"Do not conform any longer to the pattern of this world," Paul continues in verse 2, "but be transformed by the renewing of your mind. Then you will be able to test and approve what God's will is—his good, pleasing and perfect will." We are called to become *Christian non-conformists*. Our lives are to be lived in such marked contrast to the surrounding culture that the world looks upon us as peculiar, as square pegs, as people not of this broken world. While the rest of the world rushes after self-fulfillment, you and I must sacrifice ourselves for the sake of Jesus Christ.

As living sacrifices, we offer our *whole* selves, having our *whole* minds renewed, so that we can proclaim a *whole* gospel message. And what is the whole gospel? One half of the gospel is that we are called to world evangelism. The other half is that we are called to social justice. One without the other is only half a gospel. One without the other is not biblical. Jesus never intended the church to limp along on a one-legged gospel. He exemplified for us a *whole* gospel, a two-legged gospel.

Jesus not only preached the kingdom of God, He healed hurting people, He touched wounded hearts, He fed hungry people, He loved needy children. Jesus' mission must be our mission. We must preach the gospel, but we must also feed hungry children, clothe the naked, visit prisoners, and defend those who have no defense.

Over the years, Christians in different wings of the church have argued over whether the gospel is essentially spiritual or essentially social. It's not even a valid debate. The gospel is 100 percent spiritual and 100 percent social. You can't compartmentalize the gospel. You can't treat the gospel as an either/or proposition. It is a both/and proposition—spiritual and social in its implications.

It makes no sense to give a child food for one more day of physical life while withholding the food of eternal life. At the same time, if you tell her about a loving God yet demonstrate no concern over the fact that she sleeps with rats and roaches, that she has no food or clothes or education, that she's the victim of violence or sexual abuse or racism, then why should she believe your gospel? We not only have a gospel of wholeness, but we have a *whole* gospel. If we fragment that gospel into either a social or the spiritual gospel alone, then we rob the gospel of its power to change lives.

William Booth, the founder of the Salvation Army, laid down his life for the spiritual and physical needs of people. Jonathan Blanchard, the founder of Wheaton College, was an aggressive evangelist and one of the leading opponents of racism and slavery in the United States. Charles Wesley changed the course of England when he combined personal evangelism and social action in a single unified strategy. Charles Finney, often called the father of modern evangelism, took offerings for world hunger during his revival meetings.

From the earliest days of the church to such present-day Christian leaders as Billy Graham, Leighton Ford, Mark Hatfield, Charles Colson, and Anthony Campolo, we see that effective evangelism is always coupled with acts of compassion.

A number of years ago, at a Christian camp in the Midwest, I met a little girl named Tracy. She was eight years old, a child of the inner city. This was her first time at camp, and because her family was desperately poor, she had brought only one outfit for the entire week, a worn and frayed print dress. Unlike the kids who came from middle-class suburbs, Tracy brought no sleeping bag, suitcase, swimsuit, or cute short outfits— just the one faded dress she had on.

During her first few days at camp, Tracy made a

decision to receive Jesus as her Savior. Toward the end of the week, Tracy and I were talking together as we walked in the woods. "Tracy," I said, "If you could have anything you wanted, anything at all, what would you wish for?"

She was silent for a moment, giving the question a lot of thought. "Well," she said at last, "I guess I would wish I could get hit by a car. I wouldn't want to get hurt real bad—just enough so I could go to the hospital. I think it would be neat to live in a hospital."

Surprised, I said, "Why would you want to live in a hospital?"

I'll never forget Tracy's reply. "I'd like to live in a hospital," she said, "because somebody once told me that in the hospital, kids like me get three meals every day."

Three meals every day. Something you and I take for granted, yet my friend Tracy said those words in the same awed tone most people would say "a million dollars." There are so many children in the world like Tracy— children to whom three meals a day would be a dream come true. These children need to know Jesus Christ. But they also need clothes to wear and food to eat. They need someone to hug them and say, "I love you, and Jesus loves you, too."

If someone asks me, "Is the gospel spiritual or is it social?" I first think of Tracy, and then I reply, "It is both. You cannot take one dimension or the other away and have any authentic gospel left." Jesus came so that people like Tracy might have abundant life, now and forever.

As Christian non-conformists, we boldly challenge the right of this age to set the agenda for our lives. We reject the false god of Accumulation. We lay ourselves daily on God's altar, living sacrifices to the One who sacrificed Himself for us.

After all, isn't that only reasonable?

Chapter 13

—— *Hidden Riches* ——
(Romans 12:3–9)

The 1930s were hard times. On the parched plains of west Texas, the Great Depression hovered over the land like a lean vulture over a wounded jackrabbit. In the middle of this bleak land, a sheep rancher named Yates worked long hours scratching a meager existence out of the sunburned land. He divided his time between mending fences and herding his sheep from one scruffy patch of grass to the next. His land had been scoured by sandstorms and was mortgaged to the hilt. A devastating flatworm infestation had ravaged his flock. Each night after Mr. Yates trudged back to his three-room shack, his wife would serve him and his children a meal of boiled potatoes. Soon, he grimly realized, even the potatoes would run out.

Mr. Yates loved his family and he loved his land. But despair was eating away at him. He felt like a failure in the eyes of his wife and children, and in the eyes of the community. Though the Depression was hard on everyone, there was an aura of black despair about Yates that made his neighbors pity him, though they were barely surviving themselves. "Poor Mr. Yates," they called him. Yes, he was poor, all right. Dirt poor.

One day a man came onto Mr. Yates's ranch and identified himself as an oil company geologist. Mr.

Yates didn't know what a geologist was, but if the man wanted to poke around at the rocks and hardpan of his ranch, he didn't see any harm in it. A few days later, a man in a business suit came to the house with a paper for Mr. Yates to sign. Something about "mineral rights." Mr. Yates signed.

The following week, Mr. Yates watched in bewilderment as a team of men in hard-hats erected a wooden derrick on his land and began to drill. He was there when the ground rumbled, when a plug of mud shot the top off the derrick, when a black geyser of crude oil spewed 150 feet in the air. The first day's production from that well was over a thousand barrels. Within a few months, dozens of oil wells had sprung up over the rugged landscape of the Yates ranch, churning out millions of dollars for "poor Mr. Yates" and his family. After struggling for years to fend off poverty and wring a subsistence living out of the stubborn ground, Mr. Yates now saw that same land gush forth with more wealth than he had ever imagined. It had been underneath his feet all along.

This true story is a parable of the lives of many Christians today. Perhaps it is a parable of your life right now. It is a tragedy of the contemporary church that all too many Christians live in spiritual poverty, completely unaware of the riches that lie so close at hand, just waiting to be tapped. Those riches are described in Romans 12. They're called "spiritual gifts."

At this point, we come to the "hinge," the turning point in the structure of Paul's theological masterpiece, the book of Romans. Chapters 1 through 11 have dealt primarily with our *vertical* relationship with God. From Romans 12 to the end of the book, the focus now shifts to our *horizontal* relationships with others in the church, the body of Christ. The transition occurs in Romans 12:1–3. Romans 12:1 calls us to the *consecration* of ourselves as "living sacrifices" to God. Romans 12:2 calls us to *transformation*, to squarely confronting the world's effort to squeeze us into its mold. Romans 12:3 calls us to *evaluation*, to think of ourselves "with sober judgment." Here we can see a clear shift in emphasis. Whereas Romans 1–11 dealt with the great doctrines of the faith—sin, judgment, law, grace, atonement, faith—Romans 12–16 is a very down-to-earth guide to practical living among other Christians.

Many of us just love to camp in Romans 1–11, in the great doctrines of the faith. We'll gladly discuss at length the sinfulness of Man, the atoning work of Christ, the nation of Israel, or the meaning of Bible prophecy. We'll gladly show off to others how theologically astute we are. But if we are not willing to lay down our lives for other Christians, if we are not learning how to love when it's hard to love, if we are not learning to be servants in the body of Christ, then we are out of balance.

Paul begins by calling us to a realistic evaluation of who we are and how we are to live as brothers and sisters in the body of Christ. And the first dimension of ourselves that Paul calls us to evaluate is the dimension of our spiritual gifts. He writes:

> For by the grace given me I say to every one of you: Do not think of yourself more highly than you ought, but rather think of yourself with sober judgment, in accordance with the measure of faith God has given you. Just as each of us has one body with many members, and these members do not all have the same

> function, so in Christ we who are many form
> one body, and each member belongs to all the
> others. We have different gifts, according to the
> grace given us. If a man's gift is prophesying, let
> him use it in proportion to his faith. If it is
> serving, let him serve; if it is teaching, let him
> teach; if it is encouraging, let him encourage; if
> it is contributing to the needs of others, let him
> give generously; if it is leadership, let him
> govern diligently; if it is showing mercy, let him
> do it cheerfully (Romans 12:3–8).

In this passage, Paul calls us to an awareness of our spiritual gifts. It's a timely message, for the misunderstanding of this subject is directly responsible for an enormous amount of friction, frustration, and burnout in the church today. Again and again, I've seen Christians reach a place of exhaustion in their ministry for God. "I just can't handle this job," they say, "I feel like such a failure." At the same time, other Christians heap even more blame and guilt on them with remarks such as: "I always thought he was more mature than that," or, "I guess she's not as spiritual as we thought she was."

What went wrong? In many cases, a deeply committed man or woman of God was simply ministering in an area where he or she was not gifted by the grace of God, according to the teaching of Romans 12. The apostle Paul anticipated this identity crisis in the church. He knew that if we failed to understand the gifts and the roles God had given us in the church, we would end up miscast, misplaced, and misused. He understood that confusion about spiritual gifts would lead to confusion in the life and ministry of the church. So what he sets out to do in Romans 12 is to liberate us to serve as God intended.

Implied in these verses is the enormous freedom to say "No" when we are asked to take on a role or a task for which we are not gifted—and to not feel guilty about it.

Bob, a friend of mine, was a youth pastor in a large church in the Midwest. He conceived a plan for junior high ministry in which he divided the young people into groups of eight. Every group had one adult role model or mentor. They would meet with that adult mentor every week for Bible study, social activities, sporting events, and the like. Once a quarter, the group would go on a mini-retreat to a lake or to the country for a weekend of fun, relaxation, and spiritual growth. Over the course of a few years, each of these young people would be exposed to a living model of Christian character, a godly person who would teach them by word and example what it truly means to be a person of God.

Bob had a good plan—and a big job. There were several hundred junior high school students in this program, and that meant Bob had an enormous administration task on his hands: putting groups together, getting them organized, recruiting adult leaders, training those leaders, maintaining membership lists, keeping track of when each group met, and much more. So Bob found himself in the role of administrator. Just one problem: Bob didn't have the spiritual gift of administration.

Soon Bob was swamped with details he could not keep track of. He felt that the whole program was spinning out of control. He went to the pastor with his written resignation in hand. "Pastor," he said, "I can't handle this job anymore. This ministry is growing too big, too fast. I'm staying up until 2:00 in the morning working out all the details, then I go to bed and worry for another hour or two before I get to sleep. I can't take it anymore. I'm calling it quits."

But the pastor wouldn't let Bob quit. Instead, they spent the next hour together taking inventory of Bob's spiritual gifts. The breakthrough came when Bob finally realized, "Hey, I get it now! This job needs an administrator, and I don't have the gift of administration. I have the gift of teaching, the gift of showing mercy, the gift of service—but God never intended me to be an administrator."

The church set him free to express the gifts God had given him. From then on, he spent time with the young people, teaching them the Word of God and ministering with compassion to those struggling with family problems or drugs. He became enormously effective in this role, and a gifted administrator was found to run the program side of the youth ministry. Today Bob is well into his forties and still successful and effective as a youth minister—all because he discovered where his spiritual gifts truly lay.

There is no shame in admitting that we are not gifted in one area or another. When we understand where our gifts truly lie, then we have the freedom and joy of truly being the people God made us to be, doing the work God intended us to do.

This is a very personal issue to me. I've struggled in this area for many years. I know what it means to feel like a puppet, intimidated by guilt into taking on jobs in the church that I really was not suited for. And let's face it: There are people in every church who lead by intimidation, who get things done in the church by laying blame on those who don't "get with the program." Their favorite finger is an accusing index finger, and they use it to get their way in the church.

They pretend to know where you should be in the ministry of the church, and they're not a bit shy about telling you where to stand, what to do, and how to do it.

But God has given us a glorious freedom in the body of Christ to be ourselves—the special and unique selves He created us to be, with our own set of gifts and abilities. He never intended the work of the church to be carried out by intimidation.

John Knox was a man who refused to be intimidated. Known as "the Prophet of Scotland," Knox was a fiery preacher and a leader, along with Luther and Calvin, of the Protestant Reformation. Although his heart's desire was to preach the gospel and minister to the needs of the poor, he found himself thrust into the political arena in 1561 when Mary of Guise (who would later be known as Mary, Queen of Scots) arrived from France to assume the throne of Scotland. Mary was a hot-tempered Catholic, determined to stamp out the "heresy" (as she saw it) of the Reformation. Mary commanded Knox to appear for a series of "audiences"—actually verbal skirmishes in which she threatened Knox with punishment unless he abandoned his efforts to reform the Church.

But Knox refused to be intimidated. He continued to oppose the injustices and religious persecution being carried out under the reign of Mary, Queen of Scots. In response, the Queen summoned Knox to a fourth and final "audience." While awaiting his appearance, she paced in agitation, raging before her frightened counselors and courtiers about this "traitor," this "heretical preacher" John Knox. Those who heard the Queen's ravings feared for Knox's life, since a number of people (including Knox's friend and mentor George Wishart) had been burned at the stake for opposing the religious tyranny of the Crown.

The messenger dispatched to summon Knox was one of Knox's friends. He found the preacher on his knees beside his bed, deep in prayer. "John," said the messenger, "I've been sent to bring you before the Queen."

"Very well," said Knox, rising from his knees. "Let us go."

"But John," the messenger countered, "you don't understand. The Queen is in a terrible rage. I've never seen her so angry. She'd condemn you to the flames in an instant. Just say the word, and I'll tell the Queen I was unable to find you."

John Knox dusted off his knees, smiled, and said, "Why should I be afraid of a few minutes with the Queen when I've just spent four hours with the King?"

I love that response. Why should you and I ever be intimidated by those around us when we are in the presence of King Jesus? When we are secure in our own God-given uniqueness, when we clearly understand our own spiritual gifts, then we become immune to the intimidation or manipulation of others. There is an enormous sense of freedom in knowing who we are in Christ, and what gifts we've been given for God's service.

Over the years as I've spoken and taught about spiritual gifts, I've encountered six questions that I believe sum up the most common areas of misunderstanding about spiritual gifts. They are:

1. *What is a spiritual gift?* A spiritual gift is one of a variety of God-given abilities, bestowed by the Holy Spirit upon every Christian so that he or she might function effectively in the body of Christ. Spiritual gifts determine our place of ministry in the church. These gifts are given to us for our *employment*, not our

enjoyment. Though some Christians teach that each believer is given only one spiritual gift, I'm convinced that every Christian is given a number of gifts. Many Bible scholars believe the apostle Paul had at least seven spiritual gifts, and that he exercised all of them regularly.

2. *Who gives spiritual gifts?* The Giver of spiritual gifts is God. "All these [gifts] are the work of one and the same Spirit," writes Paul in 1 Corinthians 12:11, "and he gives them to each one, just as he determines." If you grasp this one principle, you will clear away probably half the confusion and misunderstanding that surrounds the subject of spiritual gifts: God gives spiritual gifts to us *just as He determines.* You and I cannot choose our gifts. We cannot read through a list of gifts and select the one gift or three gifts or five gifts we want, as if ordering from a menu.

God is sovereign. He gives gifts as He wills. This way, you and I cannot glory in our gifts. All the glory goes to God. Whatever your gifts or mine, they were given by the grace of God. Gifts are not given for our own glory, nor because we are deserving. They are tools for furthering God's kingdom.

3. *Where does the Bible teach about gifts?* There are five passages in the Bible that deal at length with spiritual gifts, as well as other verses that refer to the gifts in passing. In addition to Romans 12, spiritual gifts are listed in 1 Corinthians 12:1–11, 1 Corinthians 12:27–31, Ephesians 4:7–13, and 1 Peter 4:10–11.

Different Bible commentators have drawn slightly varying conclusions as to the precise number and meaning of the spiritual gifts listed in these passages, and some theologians would suggest that a few of the gifts listed in these passages were given for the use of the early New Testament church and are no longer given to Christians in our own time. I would encourage you to prayerfully study those passages for yourself and draw your own conclusions. From my own study, I've found the following list of spiritual gifts:

Prophecy: the ability to communicate God's message with boldness, and to call others to repentance.[1] *Service*: the ability to identify and meet needs relating to God's work. *Teaching*: the ability to communicate biblical truth to others. *Encouraging*: the ability to offer counsel to others that is comforting and challenging in a positive and healing way. *Giving*: the special ability to cheerfully contribute material resources to God's work.[2] *Leadership*: the ability to influence others to cooperate harmoniously in accomplishing the goals of God's kingdom.

Mercy: the ability to respond to the needs and hurts of others with empathy and compassion. *Helping*: the ability to increase the effectiveness of others in the church by serving in a supportive role. *Wisdom*: insight and sensitivity to the Holy Spirit's leading, which can be applied to specific issues and needs in the body of Christ. *Knowledge*: the ability to accumulate, analyze, and apply information and ideas for the betterment of the church. *Faith*: the special ability to discern God's purposes with strong confidence.[3]

Healing: the ability to serve as a human intermediary between God and those who are lacking in spiritual, emotional, or physical health. *Miracles*: the ability to serve as a human intermediary through whom God chooses to perform acts that are unexplainable according to the ordinary course of nature. *Discernment*: the ability to distinguish the right course from the wrong in times of decision. *Tongues*: the supernatural ability to speak in a language unknown to the speaker. *Interpretation*: the supernatural ability to make an utterance in tongues understood by others. *Apostle*: the ability, spontaneously and generally recognized by the church as a whole, to assume and exercise leadership in spiritual matters.

Administration: the ability to conceive and execute effective plans for carrying out the work of the church. *Evangelist*: the ability to share the gospel in such a way that others are persuaded to commit their lives to Jesus Christ. *Pastor*: the ability to provide long-term spiritual leadership and care for a fellowship of believers. *Missionary*: the ability to minister to others across the boundaries of culture and ethnicity. *Intercession*: the special ability, over and above the boundaries of most Christians, to pray regularly, frequently, effectively, and at length for the needs of others. *Hospitality*: the special ability to show generosity and welcome to strangers.

4. *What is the difference between the gifts of the Spirit and the fruit of the Spirit?* This question has puzzled many Christians over the centuries. Some people use the "gifts" and the "fruit" of the Spirit interchangeably. Yet the Scriptures make a clear distinction between the gifts of the Spirit and the nine fruit of the Spirit listed in Galatians 5:22— love, joy, peace, patience, kindness, goodness, faithfulness, gentleness, and self-control.

Whenever we come across spiritual gifts in the New Testament, we see them defined in terms of special *abilities* the Spirit gives us. No one in the body of Christ can have all the spiritual gifts, but *every* Christian should be experiencing and displaying the fruit of the Spirit in a continually growing way. The fruit of the Spirit are not abilities but *character qualities*. They are virtues that mark the life of every Christian who is becoming more mature, more Christlike as he or she lives the Spirit-controlled life. It is God's will that we be growing *not* just in one or two of the fruit of the Spirit, but in *all* of them.

Spiritual gifts are very important to God. It is clear from Romans 12 and the other Scripture passages where spiritual gifts are discussed that these gifts are absolutely essential to the ministry and functioning of the church.

At the same time, we need to understand that, as important as the gifts truly are, the *fruit* of the Spirit are vastly more important to God. He is much more interested in building character than in performing tasks. That's why Paul, after spending most of 1 Corinthians 12 talking about spiritual gifts, goes on to say, "And now I will show you the most excellent way," as he makes the transition to 1 Corinthians 13, his masterpiece on the first fruit of the Spirit—love. As we gain an overview of Scripture, we have to conclude that, while we want to discover and use our gifts for the advance of God's kingdom, we must have an even greater passion for demonstrating love in all our relationships; for expressing joy and peace; for growing in our capacity to be patient, kind, good, faithful, and gentle; for living out godly self-control.

There is no direct parallel between spiritual gifts and spiritual maturity. In fact, as we look at Scripture, we find that the most gifted church in the New Testament— the church in Corinth—was also the most spiritually immature church. It was rich in the gifts of the Spirit; it was poor in the fruit of the Spirit. As a result, this richly gifted church was rocked by division, hostility, immorality, and scandal. You can probably think of at least one modern-day version of the Corinthian church; unfortunately, I can think of many.

In my own church, when I look at the qualifications of people for ministry, I always examine that person in terms of their spiritual fruit first, their gifts second. If you carefully examine the New Testament, you will find that Paul applied the same priorities: fruit first, gifts second. In 1 Timothy 3 and Titus 1, where he sets forth the qualifications for elders or overseers in the church, Paul focuses almost exclusively on character qualities, not on abilities. He does not say, "Make sure the person you put in a leadership position has a gift of administration or giving or encouragement." Rather, he says, in effect, "Make sure you choose someone who displays unconditional love in all his relationships. Make sure that person is not quarrelsome or quick-tempered. Make sure he practices self-control." The most gifted church in the world is doomed to ineffectiveness, conflict, and chaos if its members are not daily living out the fruit of the Spirit.

5. *How do I discover my spiritual gifts?* This is probably the key question about the gifts. It is certainly the most frequently asked. And yet, as much as the Bible talks about spiritual gifts, there is not one passage of Scripture you can point to that explicitly, succinctly tells us how to discover our gifts. However, in my own study of the New Testament, I've been able to discern three ways in which we can become more aware of our gifts, and more effective in using them.

First, *be informed*. Know what the Bible says about spiritual gifts. I've known scores of people who have languished in ministry year after year, feeling frustrated, guilty, and unspiritual. In reality, their problem was simply that they failed to understand what the Bible truly teaches about spiritual gifts. When they finally discovered their own gifts and began ministering in the roles God intended for them, they began to experience the freedom that comes from living in the center of God's plan.

Second, *be open*. We need to be open to discovering gifts we never suspected we had. We should be careful not to use spiritual gifts (or a supposed lack of a certain gift) as an excuse for our laziness or lack of involvement. Many Christians skim through the lists of gifts in the Bible and hastily conclude, "Oh, I don't have that gift, nor that one, nor that one." And when they are asked to serve in the church, they glibly reply, "Oh, that's not my gift." We should be careful not to ignorantly close off an avenue of ministry God wants to open to us. We need to be open and teachable, always ready for God to disclose to us some new dimension of our personality.

When I was a teenager, after I had made my initial commitment to Jesus Christ, there was one thing of which I was absolutely certain: Whatever God wanted me to do with my life, the one thing He did not intend me to do was to become a public speaker. I was dismayed to discover I would have to take a speech class as part of my general education requirement. It was one of the most nightmarish experiences of my young adult life. I couldn't stand in front of twenty fellow students without sweating, trembling, and stammering. In fact, I was so shy that merely raising my hand in class caused my palms to sweat and my pulse to race. Any time I had a speech to give in class, I would go privately to my instructor and ask, "Is there any way

I can do independent study or a paper—*anything* so I won't have to give a speech tomorrow?" But there was never any way out.

For reasons I still do not understand, my speech instructor saw something in me that I couldn't see in myself. I was so convinced that I could never be a public speaker. My instructor kept encouraging me to look for new strengths and abilities within myself. In time, my confidence began to build, and my speaking began to improve. I joined the school debate team, and continued debating for the rest of my years in high school and college.

Today, public speaking is my principal calling in life. Among my gifts I count the gifts of a pastor and teacher. Yet there was a time when I would have thought myself more likely to pole-vault over the moon than to be a public speaker. It was not a future I was open to, but fortunately I encountered people—such as my speech instructor—who believed in me enough to *force* me to open myself to this possibility.

The strong probability is that God has given you a gift that you have not yet discovered. In fact, in your own human nature, you may be resisting that gift. God calls us to be open and teachable to the new and exciting work He wants to reveal in us.

Third, *be available*. Sometimes the only way to discover your gifts is by jumping in and meeting a need, taking on a challenge, or responding to a crisis. Sometimes the process of discovering our gifts is a matter of trial and error. One thing is certain: You will never learn what you are made of and how God has equipped you until you make yourself available to God and others in ministry.

As you become involved in service in the church, one thing is sure to happen: People will be affected. Someone will say to you, "You've really been an encouragement to me. What you said to me meant more than you'll ever know." And a realization will dawn on you: "Hey, I must have the spiritual gift of encouragement!" And that's the way it works: God gives the gifts, and our fellow believers confirm those gifts in us.

To discover our spiritual gifts, we must be available, we must get involved. You can't learn to ski by reading a book. You can't learn to swim from a correspondence course. There's no short-cut to self-understanding. The discovery of our spiritual gifts is a matter of practice, not theory.

6. *What if I fail to exercise my gifts in the body of Christ?* I've heard this question many times, and the unstated attitude behind it is this: "I'm not exercising my gifts now, and I have no interest in discovering and exercising my gifts in the future." If that is your question right now, then the issue you are really wrestling with is one of obedience to the gospel of Jesus Christ.

Romans 12 is not a "suggestion" that we use our gifts. It's a clear command. If your role in the church is that of a spectator or pew-warmer rather than a player on the field, then Paul's command is directed very pointedly at you. God did not intend His church to be a place where you could come to hear beautiful music, or a place where you could get a little motivational pep talk from the preacher once a week.

In Romans 12:4–5, Paul describes for us what God intends the church to be: a *body*. What part do you play in that body? What if God has gifted you to be the heart or the lungs of that body? What if He has gifted you to be the hands or the feet or the eyes of that body? What if you are even something so small and seemingly insignificant as an ankle?

A few years ago, I was playing basketball with a few friends. As we were playing, someone shot and missed. I jumped up to snag the rebound and landed wrong. Terrible pain shot through my ankle. X-rays later revealed a fracture. It was a very small fracture in a very small bone in a seemingly insignificant part of my body—but it left me hobbling around with my foot in a cast for weeks. It hindered my sleep at night and my activities during the day. It was just one little broken bone in my ankle, but it affected my whole body.

In the same way, you have an enormous responsibility in the body of Christ, even if you see yourself as "only an ankle." If you are not doing your part, exercising your gifts in the church, then the body is handicapped by your disobedience. The ministry of God is crippled by your inaction.

A few years ago, a pastor from another church came into my office. As we talked, his voice began to choke and tears began to spill down his cheeks. Under his leadership, the church he pastored had grown to a Sunday attendance of nearly two thousand people. Then something had gone disastrously wrong. The church had exploded in conflict over the issue of spiritual gifts. Various factions had broken away from this church. Attendance had fallen to around four hundred. The church was falling behind in its financial commitments. The whole affair had become a source of derision and embarrassment throughout the community.

"This morning," he said in a quavering voice, "I gave the board my resignation. I don't know what will happen next. I'm thinking about leaving the ministry altogether. But the worst thing of all is how this whole mess has disgraced the gospel. Our church used to be a beacon of light in the community. Now it's simply known as a church that blew apart."

The same thing could happen in my church. It could even happen in yours. You see, a spiritual gift is just a tool for doing a job. It's a lot like a hammer, a chainsaw, a butcher knife, or a lighted match. All these things are useful tools when properly and conscientiously handled. But when misused or carelessly handled, they become weapons of destruction. I've seen spiritual gifts used as weapons of destruction, too.

I suspect that's why Paul prefaces his discussion of gifts in Romans 12 with the counsel that we must consecrate ourselves as living sacrifices, that we must transform ourselves and renew our minds. He tells us not to think more highly of ourselves than we ought. The way to make sure that our gifts are used to advance rather than hinder God's kingdom is to make sure there is no jealousy or envy in our minds when we see others using their gifts.

Perhaps the most important thing to understand about gifts is our *motivation* for using them. God did not give us spiritual gifts to pump up our pride or to make us look like wonderful, talented people. The purpose of spiritual gifts is to make us more effective *servants*. When we have God's perspective on spiritual gifts, we will regard our own gifts with humility and rejoice when others discover and use their gifts. We will use our gifts as a means to love and serve one another in the body of Christ, not as an area of competition with other Christians. We will practice genuine unconditional acceptance of each other—and of each other's gifts—and we will revel in the glorious diversity of spiritual gifts being exercised within our fellowship.

God has gifted us with riches and resources beyond our imagining so that we can be the people He intended us to be, doing the work He intended us to do, ministering to the needs of our Christian brothers and sisters, and reaching a broken world for Jesus Christ. But let us keep our gifts in perspective. For in the final analysis, the world will know us as children of the living God not by our gifts but by our love.

Chapter 14

The Lifestyle of Love
(Romans 12:9–21)

Russian-born novelist Vladimir Nabokov, the author of *Lolita*, has been severely criticized as both a writer and as a human being for being cold, aloof, and lacking in compassion. One incident from Nabokov's life seems to support this assessment. It happened during the summertime shortly after World War II. While visiting friends in Alta, Utah, for a few weeks, Nabokov took daily hikes in the creek-beds and gullys outside of town. He was an avid butterfly collector, having published a number of papers on entomology, and whenever he wasn't writing he could usually be found on a butterfly-hunting expedition.

One evening after returning from his hike, Nabokov sat at the dinner table with his host and described his pursuit of one particularly interesting butterfly. "It was a *Vanessa virginiensis*," he said. "I chased the creature up the side of a steep gully. Just then I heard the most pitiful groaning from the stream below. Some careless fool with a broken leg, no doubt."

"What did you do then?" asked his host.

"What did I do?" said Nabokov blankly. "Why, I pursued the *Vanessa virginiensis*, of course. Nearly caught it, too. Gorgeous creature. The most brilliant pink and yellow markings you ever—"

"Wait," the other man interrupted, completely incredulous. "You mean you didn't stop and help the man?"

Nabokov's expression was puzzled. "Stop?" he said. "I couldn't stop. I was chasing the butterfly."

The next day, the body of an old prospector was found at the bottom of Bear Gulch. The dead man had a broken leg and had died of exposure during the night. From then on, the place was known as Dead Man's Gulch, named after the man who died because Vladimir Nabokov was busy chasing butterflies.

Unfortunately, Nabokov is not alone in his indifference to another human being's cry for help. You may recall the story of Kitty Genovese, a young New York woman assaulted, tortured, and murdered as thirty-eight people watched from their apartment windows. For an entire half-hour, she looked up at the curious faces in the apartment windows all around her, pleading for just one person to help her. No one even bothered to phone the police. Later, when police and reporters asked the apartment dwellers why they did nothing to help, the standard reply was, "I didn't want to get involved."

In Romans 12:9–13, Paul teaches us that the complete opposite of Christian love is not so much hate as *indifference*, a response to others that says, "I don't want to get involved." He writes:

> Love must be sincere. Hate what is evil; cling to what is good. Be devoted to one another in brotherly love. Honor one another above yourselves. Never be lacking in zeal, but keep your spiritual fervor, serving the Lord. Be joyful in hope, patient in affliction, faithful in prayer. Share with God's people who are in need. Practice hospitality.

I do my devotional study in a Bible I received as a gift in 1968. In preparing the material for this book, I noticed that the page containing these verses has acquired more of my own handwritten underlines, asterisks, exclamation points, and margin notes than any other page of my Bible. Pondering why this should be, I came to the conclusion that over the years, these have been strategically important verses in my life. They have transformed my Christian relationships and my ministry for Christ.

The key to understanding this passage is the recognition that these verses are not just a collection of lofty sentiments. Rather, they are God's practical, workable strategy for an effective church. These verses tell us how God expects us to live in relationship to one another. The connecting thread that wends its way through each line of this passage is *the call to involvement.*

In fact, these lines introduce the master theme of the last five chapters of Romans: the importance of our *relationships* with one another in the body of Christ. In this chapter, Paul drives home his contention that our *lifestyle of love*—our commitment to involvement in one another's lives—is what sets us apart from the rest of this broken world.

Indifference or *involvement*? Which of these two words describes your relationships with other Christians?

In our task-oriented, get-the-job-done, bottom-line culture, we easily lose sight of the fact that the purpose of the church is not to achieve goals or implement programs. The goal of the church is to glorify God and change the lives of people.

People are the most cherished resource we have in the body of Christ. People are infinitely precious, because people are the reason Jesus came to suffer and die. In an age when society is growing more and more fragmented, when love is growing cold and people are sinking into loneliness and isolation, we must affirm the biblical truth that *people* are the most precious resource we have. Our meaning and joy as human beings can only be found as we live out our lives in relationship and involvement with God and with other people.

How do we do that? What is the lifestyle of love Paul points us to in Romans 12? Clearly, he is urging us toward something more radical, more deep, more involved than merely attending church with other believers every Sunday morning. Paul has something in mind that transcends by far the superficiality and glib conversation that passes for "relationships" in western culture in the 1990s.

"Love must be sincere . . . . Be devoted to one another in brotherly love" he writes. Think about what it means to be sincerely, genuinely devoted to another person. It means to be conscious of their needs, to be committed to their care, to be willing to serve them, to be faithful in praying for them. It means to be ready to honor them, rejoice with them, or weep with them as the occasion warrants. Can you and I say with integrity that we are *devoted* to our brothers and sisters in Christ? Or do we honestly have to admit that we are really indifferent to them, to their joys and hurts and needs?

To be truly involved in the lives of our fellow Christians as God intended means that we have a special quality of relationship that is rarely found in the world anymore. Such a relationship does not take place merely as we sit in the same sanctuary with other Christians for one hour a week. Such a relationship only takes place as we open our lives to one another in a real and vulnerable way. That means we need a few settings in the church where we can have the freedom to truly be ourselves. That means we need a few Christian brothers and sisters who will keep our confidences, who will check on our personal and spiritual growth, and who will open their own lives to us.

This may take place in the setting of a regular Bible study (sometimes called a "house church," "care group," "growth group," or something similar). Or it may take place in a weekly men's prayer breakfast, where a small group of men check in with each other, sharing their struggles and praying together. Or it may take place in a women's Bible study, where Christian sisters can talk together with empathy and confidentiality, praying together for solutions to the issues they face. It may even take place in one-to-one mentoring relationships, man-to-man, or woman-to-woman.

Whatever the setting, we need a number of intimate, involved relationships in which we can say to one another, "I don't want to show you a mask or a facade. I want you to see me as I really am, including my failures, my hurts, my struggles, my brokenness, and my sin. I want to pray for you, and I need your prayers for me. I want you to hold me accountable so I can grow in those areas where there is brokenness, immaturity, or sin. I need you to help me become more like Christ." In other words, we all need relationships that are built upon a foundation of mutual *accountability*.

Accountability: Some people have a faulty notion of that word. To some it conjures up negative associations, such as legalism, or rigidity. Many Christians bear the scars of having been harshly criticized, judged, or intimidated by other Christians in the name of "accountability." Some remember having to abide by a list of do's and don'ts in the name of "accountability." Yet the fact that accountability has frequently been done badly in the church does not mean we should discard the concept altogether. Rightly practiced, accountability is a caring, nourishing, and thoroughly biblical exercise of Christian love. Most importantly, biblical accountability is the heartbeat of Paul's vision for the church in the closing chapters of Romans.

I cannot remember a single person who was in an involved and accountable Christian relationship and yet stumbled into grievous moral error, became spiritually deluded, became power-grasping and conceited, or defected from his or her faith. The person who is in the most danger from all these spiritual perils is the person who resists opening his or her life to the light, and who seeks isolation rather than involvement in his or her relationships.

We all dance at the edge of defection. We all run the risk of losing our first love for Jesus Christ. We all flirt with the lure of the world. Open, involved, accountable relationships with other Christians keep us gently in line when we are in danger of veering off course. That's why Paul, in Galatians 6:1, writes, "Brothers, if someone is caught in a sin, you who are spiritual should restore him gently. But watch yourself, or you also may be tempted."

Notice that all-important word *gently*. The purpose of accountability in our lifestyle of love is gentle restoration, not condemnation, not judgment, not harsh confrontation. There are few things more precious in this life than those special Christian brothers and sisters who love us enough to gently lead us back to Christ when we stumble. You and I need a few people in our lives who will care enough to lovingly penetrate our denials, evasions, and excuses. We need people who love us enough to hold up a mirror to our souls so we can face our spiritual condition clearly and truthfully.

If you've never been in such a relationship before, you may wonder what the lifestyle of love is like, what questions emerge in a relationship of mutual accountability. In my own life, I try to live by the counsel of Proverbs 27:6—"Wounds from a friend can be trusted." I make sure to have a few friends who will say to me, "How are you doing with your daily time of Bible study and prayer? What about those bad habits you are trying to break, and those good habits you are trying to build? What about that broken relationship you're trying to heal? Did you follow up on your decision to try to reconcile with that person? What about those priorities and commitments you made regarding your marriage and your family? Are you keeping those commitments, or have you begun to waver? How does your calendar match up with the priorities and goals you've been sharing with me?" I am asked such questions—and I ask them of my close Christian friends—at least once a week.

I know of a group of Christian businessmen in the Midwest who meet together every week. All of them are involved in executive, sales, or recruiting roles in their companies, so each of these men spends a significant amount of time traveling around the country. One week, Doug, the CEO of a manufacturing firm, mentioned to a group a struggle he was having in the area of sexual lust. "Most of the hotels I stay in have cable or satellite TV," he said, "and that means there's pornographic stuff on the tube at the touch of a button. Sometimes when I'm in that room all by myself, I think, 'Who'll know?' The first time I turned it on just out of curiosity. But sometimes I—well, the truth is, fellas, I need you guys to hold me accountable. The next time I come back from Denver or L.A. or Atlanta, I want you guys to ask me how I'm doing in this area of my life."

After Doug spoke, one of the other men, a sales rep with a publishing firm, said, "I know what you mean, Doug. And I want you to hold me accountable for the very same thing." And as the other men in the circle spoke, it became clear that Doug's struggle was a common one. But because Doug had the courage to open one dark corner of his life to the light, these men no longer had to struggle alone.

There are many forms of lust, and your area of weakness may be different from Doug's, but your need for accountable Christian relationships is no less than his. There is the lust for material things; the lust for alcohol, drugs, or over-indulgence in food; the lust for power; the lust for status; the lust for self-gratification. Someone has said, "Behavior that is observed changes." I know that's true in my life. My own accountable relationships are absolutely essential to my effort to overcome my weaknesses and temptations so I can become more like Christ.

"He who conceals his sins does not prosper," says Proverbs 28:13. The things we hide hurt us; we are only as sick as our secrets. That is both a biblical truth and a sound psychological insight. In the healing, affirming context of accountable Christian relationships, we have the freedom to share our humanness and brokenness— and it is in sharing our inner reality with other Christians that we find healing.

Are there a few people in your life who know the deepest, darkest secrets of your past, and who still love you? I've made it a priority to have such people in my life. Do you have a few friends you could call if you were in need or in the throes of depression at 3:00 A.M.? I have such friends. Do you have a few friends you could tell a secret to and know it would be held forever in confidence? I do. I have such friends because I *need* such friends. I can't live my life without them.

How do you find such friends? First, you look for people who understand and exemplify Christian love and acceptance. Second, you look for people who have integrity, people who live what they believe, even when they think no one else is looking. Third, you look for people who are godly, who want to be like Christ and who want to study God's Word. You are not looking for people who are flawless, because such people don't exist. You want to be in the company of Christians who stumble every now and then just as you do, but who have a genuine heart for God, and who want to use their mistakes to learn how to become more like Christ.

These are all qualities to look for in Christians with whom you want to build a mutually accountable relationship. But perhaps the most important way to *find* such people is to *be* such a person. Be a person of unconditional love and acceptance; be a person of integrity; be a student of God's Word, a person with a genuine desire to please God. When it is your goal to be such a friend to other people, then others with the same goals will find you. They will be drawn to you. It will be inevitable.

Tucked away in the pages of the Old Testament is a beautiful word-picture of the kind of spiritual relationship God intends you and me to experience with other believers. The setting is the desert town of Horesh, where young David hides from the murderous wrath of King Saul. Fortunately for David, he had an involved and devoted friend in the King's son, Jonathan. For in 1 Samuel 23:16, we find these words: "Saul's son Jonathan went to David at Horesh and helped him find strength in God." Jonathan sought and found David in the hills, and he encouraged and strengthened David in the Lord. Do you have a Jonathan in your life? Could you name at least one person who would go miles out of his or her way to find you and encourage you and strengthen you in the Lord if you were in need?

Several years ago, when my brother Paul was diagnosed with cancer, I flew to Denver to be with him for a few days. On returning, my wife, Shirley, met me at the airport. "Your friends in your small group Bible study are getting together tonight," she said. "They're going to have a special time of prayer for Paul and his family, and for you and our family. They know you just got back, and they don't want you to feel any obligation to come, but they wanted me to tell you they're planning to spend the entire evening in prayer."

I was touched by their involvement in my hurt. "I want to be there," I said. That night, I was covered by their love and their prayers for two solid hours. That evening was just the beginning of an experience of receiving love and strength in God from my family of faith.

A few months later, I was at Paul's bedside when he died. The very next day, three men from my church in California—three men with whom I was in a mutually accountable relationship—arrived in Denver. I hadn't asked them to come. They had simply dropped whatever business they were involved in and flew a thousand miles to be in the same city with me. Not wanting to intrude on the grief of our family, they checked into a hotel in Denver and called me at Paul's home. "Ron," they said, "we just want you to know we're here. If you need us, call us at the hotel. If you want to be alone right now, we'll just stay here." They stayed until the funeral was over, four days later.

As I think back to the way these three men and my small group Bible study and scores of others were alongside me both in prayer and in person during those days, I'm reminded of these beautiful words from the Old Testament: "Saul's son Jonathan went to David at Horesh and helped him find strength in God." And I remember those words of Paul in Romans 12: "Be devoted to one another in brotherly love."

God has called us out of isolation and indifference and into an exciting new lifestyle, the lifestyle of love. When we choose involvement in the lives of our brothers and sisters in Christ, we know that for the rest of our days, whenever we fall, we don't fall alone. We fall into the arms of love.

Chapter 15

— *The Obligation of Love* —
(Romans 13)

Step into the shoes of a plantation owner in the South. It is 1861. You've recently committed your life to Jesus Christ as your Lord and Savior. Out of your new-found faith comes a growing inner conflict: you realize that, as a slave-owner, you are morally responsible for the oppression of the scores of slaves who work on your plantation. In your conscience, there is a growing conviction that it's a sin and a social injustice for one man to enslave another. So you contact the abolitionist movement and begin arranging freedom and transportation to a free state for your slaves.

During this time, a man named Lincoln emerges as the leader of the U.S. government. You realize that his ideals have become your ideals, and you admire this man for taking a stand against slavery. Then a complication arises: Your state secedes from the Union. You are now a citizen of the Confederacy. And in Romans 13:1, you read these words: "Everyone must submit himself to the governing authorities, for there is no authority except that which God has established."

What do you do?

Now, move forward in time to the year 1935. You are an energetic, capable, patriotic citizen of Germany, and you hold a middle-ranking position in the German civil service. For two years, a man named Adolf Hitler has been the Chancellor of the government. Hitler has become aware of your talents and abilities and has just sent you a letter asking you to accept a very powerful and prestigious appointment in the government of the Third Reich.

You have a serious moral dilemma on your hands: You are aware of the hate and racism Hitler preaches, and you are a committed Christian. You want to live out your biblical beliefs in every area of your life, including your vocational life. If you accept the appointment your *Führer* offers, will you be able to practice your beliefs—or will you be compromising them? As you wrestle with this question, you turn to Romans 13:1 and read these words: "Everyone must submit himself to the governing authorities."

What do you do?

These are not theoretical situations. These are real dilemmas faced by real people, and many thousands of Christians have faced similar dilemmas over the nearly two thousand years since the book of Romans was written. It's a dilemma faced today by Christians in many countries. They turn to Romans 13 and read that Christians are to be subject to the governing authorities, and then they look at their government's policies and conclude that the governing authorities are resisting God.

How do we resolve this seeming conflict? Somehow, we must honestly grapple with the message of Romans 13 so we can understand both what it says and what it doesn't say. To do this, we must understand that no one passage of Scripture gives us all that Scripture has to say on a given topic. If we pull one verse or paragraph out of its context and say, "There it is. This is God's definitive and final word on the subject," we are deluding ourselves. We should remember the foundational principles of Bible interpretation we have received from the Reformation: Scripture interprets Scripture. Scripture affirms Scripture. Scripture validates Scripture.

As we approach Romans 13, we should keep in mind an incident from Acts 4. The apostles Peter and John are preaching the good news of the resurrected Christ to a crowd. Suddenly, they are seized and jailed by the Sadducees, who represent a combined civil-religious authority in Israel. The next day, the Sadducees bring Peter and John before the Sanhedrin, which is the ruling council of the civil-religious government. There the apostles are told to stop preaching in the name of Jesus. If Romans 13:1 were the last word on the subject, then Peter and John would be compelled to submit themselves to the governing authorities and stop preaching the gospel. But that's not what happens.

In Acts 4:19–20, Peter and John *confront* the governing authorities. "Judge for yourselves," they reply to the rulers and elders of the Sanhedrin, "whether it is right in God's sight to obey you rather than God. For we cannot help speaking about what we have seen and heard." The government was demanding that the Christian community violate the command of an even higher Authority. There is an important principle embedded in this passage: While we have a clear duty and allegiance to our government, we have an even higher allegiance to God. When Peter and John resisted the governing authority of the Sanhedrin, they did what was right in the eyes of God.

In Romans 13:2–5, Paul goes on to set forth the purpose and definition of government:

Consequently, he who rebels against the authority is rebelling against what God has instituted, and those who do so will bring judgment on themselves. For rulers hold no terror for those who do right, but for those who do wrong. Do you want to be free from fear of the one in authority? Then do what is right and he will commend you. For he is God's servant to do you good. But if you do wrong, be afraid, for he does not bear the sword for nothing. He is God's servant, an agent of wrath to bring punishment on the wrongdoer. Therefore, it is necessary to submit to the authorities, not only because of possible punishment but also because of conscience.

The purpose of government, says Paul, is to be a terror to evil. But when government becomes a terror to good, when it resists God and perpetuates evil and injustice, then government must be opposed. Human governmental authority exists for good reason, but there is always a higher authority than human authority, and that is God Himself.

But there's a catch here. We should never assume that there is no price to pay for our allegiance to God. It is often a costly thing to obey God rather than human authority. We must be willing to accept those consequences.

Consider this scenario: A Christian high school student is in a class entitled "Sex Education." The self-styled "progressive" teacher of the class has brought a pornographic videotape to show the class as part of the curriculum. What does the Christian student do?

First, if he wants to be true to his Christian principles, he raises his hand. Gently but persistently, he voices his conscientious objection to the showing of the pornographic film. He is not rude, contentious, abrasive, or insulting to his teacher. Rather, he is gentle and respectful, for he is seeking to project the gentleness and humility of his Lord Jesus Christ.

If the teacher insists on showing the film, the student then persists in his objections. "I would like to be excused from this class," he says, "because my Christian conscience does not permit me to view this film." If the teacher again refuses and proceeds with the showing of the videotape, the student again objects. By now, of course, the teacher is likely to be annoyed, if not downright livid, with our young Christian friend. The teacher may say, "All right! If you want out of this class, then go to the principal's office. But understand that if you walk out that door, you get an automatic F in this class."

Now the student is confronted with the fact that there is a price to pay for following his conscience and his Lord. But if he is true to his principles, he will reply, "Thank you for excusing me from the class. I'll go to the principal's office and I'll accept whatever grade or discipline you decide to give me. But I continue to insist that what you are doing is wrong, and I can't be a part of it."

You may think, "That's an outrageous scenario. Such things don't really happen. There are no teachers showing pornographic films in the classroom." But this is not an imaginary scenario. This event actually happened in an American public school, as reported on Dr. James Dobson's *Focus on the Family* radio series. And as a result of one student's courageous witness, many lives and hearts in that community were changed, as well as the sex education policies of the school district.

How do we discern whether authority is to be obeyed or challenged? Bible scholar Charles Ryrie makes this observation: "When civil law and God's law are in opposition, the illustrations of the Bible sanction, if not obligate, the believer to protest, if not disobey. But when a believer feels he should disobey his government he must be certain it is not because the government has denied him his rights, but because it has denied him God's rights." In other words, the disobedience of civil authority is justified at the point when authority demands we disobey God—and not until that point.

I know many well-meaning people, Christians and non-Christians, who are ready to oppose the government whenever its policies conflict with their personal views or whenever they feel their rights have been violated. Yet I would suggest that the issue of submission versus disobedience to authority hinges not on "my" rights, but on *God's* rights. We know we must disobey government at the point when allegiance to the government would cause us to violate our allegiance to God.

This is not a theoretical issue. It is a very real and contemporary issue. My friend Kevin Ford recently told me of a woman he knows in a European communist country who made a commitment to Christ at an evangelistic meeting. As she raised her hand in that meeting, she knew she was being observed by the authorities and that her career as a public school teacher was over at that moment. Yet, even more than she wanted her job, she wanted to submit to God.

Two members of the pastoral staff of my church were arrested and later released for witnessing for Jesus Christ in an eastern European country. Another friend of mine, who is currently a missionary in the Middle East, spent eight months in a Libyan prison for distributing Christian literature there. He told me that when Muslims in most Middle Eastern and North African countries convert to Christianity, they risk imprisonment, torture, and death at the hands of the religiously-dominated government.

There are scores of similar stories that can be told about Christians in places like South Africa, Cuba, the Soviet Union, China, and elsewhere. Such stories are even unfolding in America, where many loyal, law-abiding Christians who deeply love their country find that they must gently but persistently resist the government in its official sanction of indiscriminate abortion.

Martin Niemoller was a German pastor and theologian, and one of the founders of the Anti-Nazi Confessing Church during Hitler's rule. He openly opposed Hitler's racist policies and the government's attempts to control the churches in Germany. In 1937, Niemoller was arrested by the Gestapo. He was confined in such prisons as Sachsenhausen and Dachau until he was freed by the Allies in 1945.

During his imprisonment, one of Niemoller's friends, another pastor, visited him in prison. "Martin, if you had just kept your mouth shut, you would be a free man. Have you forgotten Romans 13:1? Have you forgotten that Paul wrote that we should submit ourselves to the governing authorities? What in the world are you doing in this prison?"

Niemoller looked his well-meaning friend squarely in the eyes and said, "I think the real question is, Why in the world aren't you in this prison with me?"

In Matthew 22:21, Jesus says, "Give to Caesar what is Caesar's, and to God what is God's." But when Caesar takes what rightfully belongs to God, we have no choice but to disobey. Christians are to set the pace as model citizens of the community and of the nation. God calls us to pay our taxes, to be informed about governmental policies and social issues, to vote responsibly, and to be salt and light—a preservative and a source of illumination—in our world. But when government does evil or asks us to do things that are evil, then we must obey the higher government of the kingdom of God, where our true citizenship and allegiance ultimately lies.

In Romans 13:6–10, Paul makes a transition from our obligation to the government to our obligation to one another in the body of Christ, and in the human family as a whole. He writes:

> This is also why you pay taxes, for the authorities are God's servants, who give their full time to governing. Give everyone what you owe him: If you owe taxes, pay taxes; if revenue, then revenue; if respect, then respect; if honor, then honor.
>
> Let no debt remain outstanding, except the continuing debt to love one another, for he who loves his fellowman has fulfilled the law. The commandments, "Do not commit adultery," "Do not murder," "Do not steal," "Do not covet," and whatever other commandment there may be, are summed up in this one rule: "Love your neighbor as yourself." Love does no harm to its neighbor. Therefore love is the fulfillment of the law.

Many of my Christian friends have looked at these verses and have concluded that it's wrong to borrow money. They refuse to take out a loan on a car, obtain a mortgage for a house, or own a credit card. "Let no debt remain outstanding," they quote. And while I respect the good intentions of these well-meaning friends, I don't believe that is what Paul is telling us in Romans 13. In the original Greek, he uses the continual present tense, which suggests that what he is really saying is, "Don't develop a lifestyle where you are continually owing people money. Pay your bills."

The more significant dimension of Paul's teaching in this passage is: "Let no debt remain outstanding, *except the continuing debt to love one another*, for he who loves his fellowman has fulfilled the law." The real thrust of Paul's teaching is that we have an ongoing debt, a continual obligation of love. This is what we owe to every human being with whom we come in contact: the obligation of unconditional Christian love. For when we love our neighbor, we fulfill God's law.

As we take a close look at this passage, an interesting fact emerges. In the New International Version (quoted above), we see that the word "neighbor" appears twice. Yet if you search the original Greek text of these verses, you do not find the Greek words for "neighbor." Instead, you find the Greek word *heteros*, which translated literally means "the other." It connotes a person who is different from us.

What is Paul getting at? I believe Paul deliberately chose a word that would penetrate our tendency to only love those who are similar to ourselves. He is saying that we are to learn to love the *heteros*, the other, the person of a different background, different race, different social and economic status from our own. We are even to love those with different opinions, ideas, and values from our own. That means we are to learn to love even when it's hard to love. We must learn to accept people even when their doctrine, their personality, or their politics is hard to accept.

Paul's message in Romans 13 runs counter to the attempts of many Christians who champion the cause of homogeneous, target-audience, demographically-focused churches. There are people in Christendom today who believe each church should decide who its "audience" is and how to "grab" that audience. Churches would then be able to make a statement such as, "Our ministry is to white suburban couples in their thirties with an average of 1.6 children."

But Paul, in Romans 13, tells us we are to be a heterogeneous church, a church that owes a debt of love to the *heteros*, to the person who is different from us. That means we are going to demonstrate acceptance and love to married people, single people, divorced people, the elderly, whites, blacks, hispanics, Asians, native Americans, the wealthy and powerful, the homeless and powerless, people with physical or mental impairments, people recovering from addictions, professional people, blue-collar people, Ph.D.s and M.D.s, people without education, Democrats, Republicans, people from different denominational backgrounds, people with different beliefs, people who are as unlike ourselves as night is different from day. We will welcome all these *heteros* others into our fellowship and into our lives because we owe them a debt, an obligation of love.

Moreover, says Paul (echoing Leviticus 19:18 and the words of Jesus in Matthew 22:39), we fulfill God's law when we love our neighbor *as we love ourselves*. Some of us in the Christian church are uncomfortable with the idea of loving ourselves. We rightly reject the self-adulation and self-fascination that so characterizes our society in the 1990s. As a result, we are puzzled by the idea that we should love others as we love ourselves. We would be more comfortable if the Bible said, "Love your neighbor as you love your own family" or, "Love your neighbor as you love God." But that's not what the Bible says.

In these verses, we have stumbled onto a beautiful paradox of the Christian faith. For the amazing truth about ourselves is that—even though we are sinners, even though we are unworthy—God gave His Son Jesus to die for us. Because of the sacrificial work of Jesus, God now views us not as unworthy sinners but as a royal priesthood, a chosen people, children of the living God, bearers of His image. Our bodies are the temple of the Holy Spirit, and collectively we are the body of Christ on earth. We have received unique gifts from the Spirit. Do you begin to see in this description of ourselves a basis for biblical self-love?

A number of years ago, when I was on the pastoral staff of a church in Minneapolis, the church had a telephone ministry in which people could dial up a recorded two-minute devotional. This number averaged around a hundred calls per day, and the members of our pastoral team would take turns recording a new message each morning. Our daughter, Rachael, was about four at the time. Some mornings I brought Rachael with me and she would say a poem or sing a song for the recording. I'll always remember the words of one song she used to sing:

> I'm a special person.
> There's no one like me.
> I'm so glad I'm Rachael.
> That's my name, that's me.
> God thinks I'm special.

He thinks you are special, too.
And I'm so glad that I'm me
And you are you.

That's a beautiful, simple statement of what it means to love yourself as God intends. That's the kind of biblical self-love we should be building into ourselves, our children, and those around us.

When our son, Nathan, was about five or six years old, I used to play a little relational game with him every now and then at bedtime. I would ask him, "Nate, if you could be anybody else in the world, who would you be?" And Nathan always had the same answer: "If I could be anybody in the world, I'd be me." "Why would you be you?" I would ask. And he would say, "Because I like me."

That's a liberating truth. When we see ourselves as God sees us and love ourselves as God loves us, then we become empowered to release that same kind of love toward others. "Love your neighbor as yourself," is God's counsel to us in the Old Testament, in the words of Jesus, in the words of Paul.

Romans 13 is a chapter of obligations. We are obligated to be citizens of our country, but we are first and foremost obligated to the kingdom of God. We are obligated to pay what is due, whether taxes, respect, or honor. And there is one obligation that we owe to every other human being we meet, a debt of love, an obligation to unconditionally accept and seek the welfare even of those who are completely different from ourselves. And that's not easy, is it?

It's not easy to love that man in your church with the abrasive, pushy personality. It's not easy to love the sharp-tongued, bossy woman on the Fellowship

Committee. It's not easy to love that next-door neighbor who throws loud backyard parties until 2:00 in the morning. It's not easy to love the boss who continually berates you and criticizes your work. It's not easy to love the teenager who was caught vandalizing your home. It's not easy to love that parent-in-law who has never accepted you or gotten along with you. It's not easy—but in God's strength it is possible.

The key to understanding these closing chapters of Romans is to realize that Paul has not written a series of idealistic but hopelessly impractical little homilies. The goals Paul outlines for us in these chapters are attainable goals as we yield our lives to the Holy Spirit. And the primary goal Paul sets before us is that we are to love the other person, that person of a different kind, in the same way we love ourselves. For when we do that, we are well on our way to fulfilling the law of Christ.

Chapter 16

The Strong and the Weak
(Romans 14)

Long before I had my first official pastorate, even before I went to seminary, I was hired to be the preacher of a little church in rural Iowa. I was only eighteen years old, a freshman at Iowa Western College. The fifty-or-so members of this church met in a white clapboard church building surrounded by fields of corn, just about five miles from my hometown. To this day, I marvel that those big-hearted Iowa farm-people were so gracious as to endure my first attempts at preaching during the eight months I was with them.

The people of that little church held to all the same essential doctrines of the Christian faith that I did. Yet they also held a number of convictions that were very different from the convictions that I had been raised in. They believed, for example, that it's wrong to sing hymns, since hymns might contain poor theology or might have been written by ungodly people. The church had no piano, no organ, and certainly no guitars. As a matter of conviction and conscience, these people had no music in their worship services except the Psalms. Every Sunday, in addition to preaching, I led the congregation a cappella from *The Psalter*, a book containing all 150 Psalms set to music.

These people also believed Sunday should be called the Sabbath. On the Sabbath you were expected to worship in the morning, rest with your family in the afternoon (preferably by reading the Bible), then return to church in the evening for another worship service. This was certainly not a bad custom, but it was observed with a sense of strict obligation that was not part of my own church background.

I could go on and list dozens of convictions they held that were foreign to my own heritage and beliefs. I was troubled as to how to deal with this situation. I felt these people had unnecessarily bound themselves with rules and legalistic observances. Didn't they know about the freedom they had in Jesus Christ? At the same time, I thought to myself, *Here I am, a young man in the pulpit for the first time, only eighteen years old. What right do I have to try to change the way these people believe?*

After a few weeks of indecision, I went to my father for advice. He had spent most of his life pastoring a church in Iowa, and I knew he would bring a wise perspective to the situation. After explaining the convictions of my congregation to my dad, I asked, "What do you think I ought to do, Dad?"

He replied, "You should honor and respect and encourage the convictions of your people." As years have gone by, I've come to appreciate my father's advice more and more. He was saying, in essence, exactly what the apostle Paul says to us in Romans 14. Paul writes:

> Accept him whose faith is weak, without passing judgment on disputable matters. One man's faith allows him to eat everything, but another man, whose faith is weak, eats only

vegetables. The man who eats everything must not look down on him who does not, and the man who does not eat everything must not condemn the man who does, for God has accepted him. Who are you to judge someone else's servant? To his own master he stands or falls. And he will stand, for the Lord is able to make him stand.

One man considers one day more sacred than another; another man considers every day alike. Each one should be fully convinced in his own mind. He who regards one day as special, does so to the Lord. He who eats meat, eats to the Lord, for he gives thanks to God; and he who abstains, does so to the Lord and gives thanks to God. For none of us lives to himself alone and none of us dies to himself alone. If we live, we live to the Lord; and if we die, we die to the Lord. So, whether we live or die, we belong to the Lord.

Here, Paul divides the church into two groups, which he calls the strong and the weak. The weak are those who feel they cannot eat meat, those who feel obligated to observe the Sabbath and other special days, those who feel the need for more formal rules and restrictions in their religious life. The strong are those who have a greater sense of freedom in the Christian faith.

It's clear which side Paul identifies with, because in Romans 15:1 he writes, "We who are strong ought to bear with the failings of the weak . . . ." Paul was personally on the side of the strong. Paul had no convictions against eating meat. He felt great freedom from having to observe a set of restrictions about the Sabbath. Yet Paul displays nothing but respect for those who hold differing convictions from his own. Paul's acceptance of those who differ with him contrasts with the mentality of so many Christians today, a mentality that is summed up in these lines I came across a few years ago.

> Believe as I believe, no more, no less.
> That I am right, and no one else, confess.
> Feel as I feel, think only as I think.
> Eat what I eat, drink only what I drink,
> Look as I look, do always as I do.
> Then, and only then, will I fellowship with you.

Christians divorce themselves from other Christians over a variety of issues. Christians who don't dance, drink alcohol in moderation, play cards, or go to certain movies judge those who do. Those who do those things judge those who don't. Christians judge their fellow Christians for being politically liberal or politically conservative; for driving a luxury car; for being in a trade union; for a whole host of reasons that have little or nothing to do with a person's love for Jesus or the moral quality of his or her life.

In Paul's day, the attitudes and problems in the church were similar to those of our day, but the issues were different. One issue Paul mentions in Romans 14 is the eating of meat. You may wonder why there should be division in the early church between vegetarians and meat-eaters.

The problem can be traced to the fact that much of the meat that was sold in the markets of Paul's world was from animals slaughtered and sacrificed to pagan idols. Usually only a portion of each sacrificial animal was burned as an offering, and the rest of the carcass was sold in meat markets that were often adjacent to the pagan temples. Many Christians had a conscientious objection to eating meat that had been butchered in the process of a pagan religious rite, feeling that to do so would be to condone and support a false religion. So Paul's counsel to those who felt no twinge of conscience over the issue of eating meat is like the counsel I received from my father: "When you eat with other Christians, you honor and respect and encourage the convictions of your brothers and sisters in Christ."

Another issue in the church of Paul's era was the issue of special calendar days. Most early Christians, having come out of a background of Judaism, brought with them a deep desire to honor the Sabbath and other holy days. They understood that the Christian faith did not mean the cancellation of Judaism, but its fulfillment. Over the hundreds of years of Jewish history and tradition, the Sabbath and other Jewish feast days had become surrounded by hundreds of rules and regulations. So it was only natural that many newly converted Jewish Christians wanted to continue to honor the Sabbath and other holy days as they had been taught within Judaism—rules and all.

So the apostle Paul, addressing the Christians at Rome, says in effect, "When another Christian comes to church to worship alongside you, and he believes in honoring the holy days according to Jewish tradition, you honor and respect and encourage the convictions of your brother or sister in Christ." What Paul wants us to understand as members of the body of Christ is that there is a far more profound issue at stake than whether or not to eat meat or observe ancient traditions. What is at stake here is how we treat one another and love one another and honor one another in the body of Christ.

Paul's theme in Romans 14 is what today we would

call "gray areas." These are the amoral areas, issues in which no clear-cut, black-and-white command has been given in the Bible. As we approach those issues where no biblical absolutes are involved, each of us must seek the guidance of the Holy Spirit in arriving at our convictions. Each of us will approach these "gray areas" in different ways, coming to different conclusions. And each of us must live out our own obedience to God in our own unique way. The apostle Paul is deeply concerned that as we arrive at our own convictions we guard against self-righteousness, and against a judgmental spirit.

Some years ago, a woman was talking with me about some areas of disagreement she had with her husband. These disagreements were causing severe tensions in their marriage relationship. With complete seriousness and sincerity she summed up the conflict between them as she saw it: "Whenever we have an argument, my husband goes his way and I go God's way." She was utterly convinced that, even in issues where the Bible is silent, her way was God's way, and her husband was dead wrong. Paul, in Romans 14, issues a strong warning against such an attitude.

The issue, to Paul, is not rules or dogmas or convictions. The issue is *attitude.* To the strong Christian, the believer who is secure in his Christian freedom, he says in effect, "If you *really* understand grace and freedom, then don't ever use that freedom in a self-righteous way. Don't ever flaunt your freedom. Don't ever belittle someone who doesn't understand Christian freedom yet. Don't judge, don't ridicule."

Let's fast-forward Romans 14 to the 1990s and put this teaching in a cultural context that you and I can identify with, beginning with the issue of alcohol. And let's be candid: The use of alcohol is viewed differently within different denominations and in different parts of the country. Many Christians take the position that having a glass of wine with dinner is a sin, while others, who are no less committed to Jesus Christ, take a much more relaxed view of drinking.

I've been around some of these "liberated" Christians who, seeing themselves as the strong Christians in Romans 14, will gather together with a glass of wine or a mixed drink in their hands while making fun of those poor legalists who just aren't freed up enough in their faith to know that it's okay to drink. Frankly, I'm very weary of that kind of "Christian freedom." I'm weary of those who flaunt their freedom and belittle their teetotaler brothers and sisters, because underneath the jokes, there's an attitude of self-righteousness, judgmentalism, and arrogance. It's an attitude that says, "I've grown beyond that legalistic phase in my Christian maturity."

Jerry is a Christian friend of mine who used to joke about his abstaining brothers and sisters. Jerry doesn't joke about them anymore. Not long ago, I visited Jerry in the chemical dependence treatment unit of a hospital. Jerry thought he was a strong Christian, as described in Romans 14, but his "strength" turned out to be a serious weakness.

But Paul doesn't reserve his warnings for the strong alone. He turns to the weak, to those with strict convictions in the gray areas of the faith, and he says in effect, "You have your convictions and that's fine. Do as the Holy Spirit leads you. But make sure you don't ever hold your convictions like a club over your Christian brother or sister. Make sure you don't ever judge your fellow Christian for not sharing your convictions."

This principle applies not only in the church but in

our families. As parents, we pray for wisdom every day because we want to impart Christian values and Christian maturity to our children. Yet we easily lose sight of what are essential Christian values and what are the "gray areas," the peripheral issues of our faith. In our eagerness to pass on our faith to our children, we may risk attempting to clone our children in our own image rather than enabling them to grow into the likeness of Christ. Even though our children are sincerely seeking Christ in their lives, we may find their taste in clothes and music, their political beliefs, and their way of expressing themselves to be alien to some of our own tastes. And we have a tendency, sometimes, to confuse matters of taste or conviction with matters of scriptural absolutes. When that happens, the stage is set for potentially destructive conflict.

A good analogy for raising a child is flying a kite. Kite-flying is an art, a delicate process of sensing when to let out a little more string, when to tug the kite against a falling wind. Too little string, too much freedom too soon, and the kite can get away from us or can snag a tree.

If we teach our children Christian responsibility, if we teach them to use their own minds and to be sensitive to the leading of the Holy Spirit, it is as if we are gently, sensitively playing out string for our kite. How much string do you let out for your child at six? At twelve? At seventeen? Kite flying is a delicate business, and it requires discernment, sensitivity, and a little experimentation. The object of kite-flying, remember, is not to clutch the kite to our bosom, nor to release the kite and watch it soar out of sight and beyond recovery. The object is to watch it fly. And a flying kite does unexpected things. It bobs and dips and weaves in patterns that we can neither predict nor control. That's as it should be.

A kite must seek its own way among the winds. A child must find his or her own set of convictions. If you want to bring disharmony and conflict into your home, then one of the best ways I know is to try to control your child's thinking and behavior in the "gray areas," the non-essential areas, the issues on which there is no firm biblical counsel. But if you want to build a lasting, harmonious relationship with your child, the best thing you can do is to give your child the appropriate amount of freedom and the right to be different from you in those "gray areas."

Now, why does Paul spend an entire chapter of Romans dealing with this issue of the strong and the weak? He gives us a clue in verses 7 and 8: "For none of us lives to himself alone and none of us dies to himself alone . . . . Whether we live or die, we belong to the Lord." The seventeenth-century poet John Donne echoes these words of Paul when he writes, "No man is an island, entire of itself; every man is a piece of the continent, a part of the main." This issue is important to Paul, first, because he wants us to understand that we are all inter-related and inter-dependent in the body of Christ. We are all part of each other. And that means our relationships and our love for one another far outweigh the importance of those "gray areas" that so easily divide us.

The issue is important to Paul, second, because he wants us to understand that we are all members of the same body under the same head. "If we live," he says, "we live to the Lord; and if we die, we die to the Lord. So, whether we live or die, we belong to the Lord." When we lose that perspective, then we begin to view Christians who differ from us in this or that detail as a bit suspect. We begin to question their sincerity, their genuineness, because their convictions don't match up with ours. That's why, in verse 4, Paul says, "Who are you to judge someone else's servant? To his own master he stands or falls." We have no right to judge or reject someone God has accepted.

And this issue is important to Paul, third, because we must all, as Christians, face the same judgment. Not a judgment for sin, because that was dealt with once and for all by Jesus on the cross. But Paul writes, verse 10, "You, then, why do you judge your brother? Or why do you look down on your brother? For we will all stand before God's judgment seat." Here Paul reveals that there will be a second judgment, apart from the judgment for sin, in which we will account to God for the way we have lived as members of the body of Christ. And we will not be evaluated on the basis of whether we ate meat or observed certain calendar days, but on the attitudes we harbored toward those who differed with us in the "gray areas."

When I was a college freshman, I dated a high school senior named Marilyn. She was a Christian, raised in a different church than I was, and it was part of her convictions that she should not go to any movies, nor play cards, nor dance. You might think that such a "straight-laced" mentality might mark her out as one of the dreariest, least popular girls in school. You'd be wrong. Because of Marilyn's pleasing, outgoing personality and vivaciousness, she was always surrounded by friends. In fact, in her senior year, she was elected homecoming queen.

This presented an interesting problem for Marilyn, for the tradition at this high school was that the homecoming queen was crowned at the homecoming dance. Immediately after the queen was crowned, she and her escort would dance one dance especially in her honor. But Marilyn believed it was wrong for a Christian to dance. So Marilyn proposed a solution to the homecoming committee that was eagerly accepted. After she was crowned, an announcer came to the microphone and said, "In honor of Queen Marilyn, the queen's attendants and their escorts will dance." Marilyn watched the dance in her honor, but she neither participated in the dance nor did she judge those who did. I respected and admired that.

But what if Marilyn had decided to do what was traditionally expected of the homecoming queen? What if she had chosen to dance? In Romans 14:23, Paul uses meat-eating as an analogy to illustrate how we should respond to life's "gray areas." He writes, ". . . the man who has doubts is condemned if he eats, because his eating is not from faith; and everything that does not come from faith is sin." Thus, if someone has convictions about not eating meat, yet because of peer pressure or some other reason he goes ahead and eats, then that is sin for that person—even if eating meat is *not* sin for the next person. Similarly, if Marilyn had chosen to dance as the homecoming queen, then that would have been sin for her, even if it was not a sin for every other person in that room.

The spiritual principle embodied in Romans 14:23 may seem paradoxical and even illogical to you. We are accustomed to thinking that "sin" is a list of activities, and all we have to do to live a righteous life is avoid doing all the things on the "sin" list. And of course, there is a list of sins, a list of activities, that are always wrong no matter what the circumstances. It's called the Ten Commandments. But surrounding the Ten Commandments is a cloud of "gray" activities, amoral activities. Each of us must search his or her own heart and come to a point of conviction regarding these "gray areas." And if we transgress our convictions, we commit sin.

Life is full of such "gray area" choices. Dancing is one. The use of alcohol is another. For single people, the area of courtship and sexual expression is another. The Bible is clear on the fact that sexual intercourse outside of marriage is sin. But what about other forms of intimate activity—kissing, touching, the kinds of things that are said between people in love? Where—as the Holy Spirit leads you and convicts you—do you draw the line?

What about the way you dress? Women in particular have a range of difficult choices to make, for ours is a culture that advertises women's clothing as weapons of seduction. As a Christian, you have been given great freedom to dress any way you want to dress; you will find few specific guidelines in Scripture on the subject. But how do you want to dress as a person who belongs to Christ? As the Holy Spirit leads you and convicts you, where do you draw the line?

There are so many other "gray areas" where difficult choices must be made: Is it right, in light of Scripture and the enormous spiritual and social needs in the world, for us to purchase that expensive stereo or video system? That luxury car? That palatial home? Is it ethical to be involved in certain business ventures? Should I, as a Christian businessman, be seen in a restaurant having lunch with a female colleague or client? Am I going to offend a Christian brother or sister if I am seen walking into this theater or that concert?

There is a step-by-step process by which we can

determine whether or not we should engage in a given "gray area" activity. (1) We ask ourselves, "Is this issue addressed in Scripture?" If not, we proceed to the next step. (2) We ask ourselves, "Do I believe, as a matter of conscience and by the conviction of the Holy Spirit, that it is all right for me to engage in this activity?" If the answer is no, then that ends the matter; to engage in this activity would be sin. But if the answer is yes, then we still have one more step to take. (3) We ask ourselves, "How will my involvement in this activity affect others?"

In verse 20, Paul writes, "Do not destroy the work of God for the sake of food. All food is clean, but it is wrong for a man to eat anything that causes someone else to stumble." Remember that Paul uses the specific example of food to illustrate a broader principle. Today he might say, "Don't destroy the work of God for the sake of a too-revealing dress or a movie or a luxury car or an alcoholic beverage. Don't do anything that causes another person to stumble."

This principle could be summed up in three words: *Love limits liberty.* We live under grace. We have enormous freedom as Christians, but sometimes we must limit our freedom to show love to others.

As Christians, we readily accept the fact that refraining from sin is our duty. What is harder for some of us to accept is that refraining from "gray area" activities—activities that God has given us complete freedom to engage in—is our demonstration of Christian love. There are many things we are free to do but that we choose not to do if we truly love our brothers and sisters in Christ.

When that kind of love is our goal, then we become even more identified with our Lord Jesus, who (as Paul tells us in Philippians 2) had all the freedom, power, and prerogatives of God, yet who humbled Himself, who in love chose to limit His liberty, who took the form of a servant and gave himself as a sacrifice for you and me.

If we could boil Romans 14 down to a single sentence, I think it might be this: The best way to live out our Christian freedom is by knowing we have it without taking every opportunity to use it. You and I are free in Christ. And there is nothing in the world that can limit our freedom but our love for God and our love for one another.

Chapter 17

How's Your A.Q.?
(Romans 15)

A few years ago, Romans 15 came true in the life of a church on the West Coast. It happened during a Sunday morning worship service. The church was located near a college campus, and many students attended on Sunday mornings. Most of these students dressed informally and practiced a relaxed style of worship. They thought of the "old-timers" in the church as rigid and archaic.

The older parishioners, however, tended toward conservatism in their theology, politics, dress, and social values. They believed in traditional modes of worship and viewed the young people with suspicion. These differences were a source of growing tension in the church.

One Sunday morning, a young man came into the service during the second hymn. He was dressed as if he had just beamed down from another galaxy. There were streaks of fluorescent orange in his hair and an earring dangled from one ear. He walked up the center aisle to the front of the sanctuary, scanning the pews for a place to sit. The pews, however, were full, so he simply sat down in the aisle next to the first pew.

Looking up from their hymnbooks, gray-haired men in charcoal suits and black ties frowned. White-haired matrons in silk dresses and white gloves sniffed their disapproval.

213

Then one of the deacons, a dignified looking man in his eighties, rose from his seat in the back of the sanctuary, steadied himself on his cane, and began to walk slowly up the center aisle. His eyes were fixed on the back of the young man's head.

The hymn ended, and the congregation sat down. Around the sanctuary, eyes shifted apprehensively to the elderly gentleman as he reached the place where the young man sat in the aisle. Everyone seemed to be awaiting the inevitable confrontation, and no one knew how to avert it.

The deacon bent slightly, gripping his cane, and put one hand on the young man's shoulder. The entire congregation held its breath. Then the deacon slowly eased himself down onto the carpet, joining the young man in the aisle. The two of them now sat cross-legged together, side-by-side on the floor.

And there was the sound of sniffling and the sight of lacy white handkerchiefs being dabbed at many eyes as the pastor stepped into the pulpit and said, "What I am about to preach you will probably forget. But what you have just seen, you will always remember."

This was a church that had learned a lesson in *acceptance*. In Romans 15, Paul writes:

> May the God who gives endurance and encouragement give you a spirit of unity among yourselves as you follow Christ Jesus, so that with one heart and mouth you may glorify the God and Father of our Lord Jesus Christ. Accept one another, then, just as Christ accepted you, in order to bring praise to God.

If we are to be people of God, then we must be people of *acceptance*. We will live out our lives with an attitude of acceptance toward those who are different, hurting, disadvantaged, or broken by sin. When we do so, we mirror to others the acceptance God has so graciously shown to us—and that brings praise to God.

The opposite of acceptance is prejudice, and thus God calls us to face our prejudices and eliminate them. Not too many of us will admit to being prejudiced—but if we are honest, most of us would have to admit that at one time or another we have made such statements as:

"Poor people are just lazy!"

"I never met a rich man who wasn't crooked!"

"He's just been released from prison and the pastor wants us to take him into our Bible study group, but, well, I just don't trust him."

"Young people today! Don't you think someone who dresses like that must be on drugs?"

"How can a liberal Democrat call himself a Christian?"

"He's a conservative Republican. How can any intelligent person hold such views?"

"She's not the right kind of person for this committee position. Didn't you know she's been seeing a psychiatrist?"

"I don't know the medical term, but he had some kind of breakdown a couple years ago. Isn't there someone else who'd be better suited for the job?"

I'm not suggesting we cannot have honest differences with one another over doctrines, values, issues, or interpretation of Scripture. We must mix freely with people from different perspectives. The question is: Are we going to be *accepting* of those with whom we differ—or will we allow those differences to produce bitterness and division?

A number of years ago, I knew a young man who was a casualty in his church. I call him a casualty because he had once been very active in his youth group, and he seemed very committed to Christ. Suddenly he dropped out of church and became involved in a cult, a religious group centered around an authoritarian leader, unbiblical doctrines, and bizarre practices. Several people in the church sought unsuccessfully to bring him out of that cult and back into their own fellowship. They questioned him about the teachings of the cult and tried to get him to examine his newfound beliefs in light of the Bible.

They found, however, that his reasons for joining the cult had nothing to do with doctrines or logic or truth. It had to do with *acceptance*. "Look," he said, "I don't really care what the people in this group teach. I don't really understand all their beliefs, or how they differ from what you believe in your church. All I know is that when I was going to church with you, I felt I didn't fit in. I felt you were all looking down on me because of my clothes and my background. But in my new church—which you call a 'cult'—I'm *accepted*."

Truly, the deciding issue for most people when they are looking for a place of belonging is not orthodoxy, but *acceptance*. In fact, genuine orthodoxy—that is, genuine adherence to the revealed truth of the Bible—is expressed in loving, caring action, not merely in words, rules, and ideas. As Elton Trueblood has observed, "The unloving fellowship is an heretical fellowship, so far as Christianity is concerned. How strange, in light of the biblical insistence on love as the principal thing, that we have emphasized it so little in comparison with other elements . . . . Love is the final test of orthodoxy.[1]

My friend Dave has found it difficult to find a church family that practices an orthodoxy of love. The reason is that Dave has struggled for most of his life with a confused sexual identity. In his late adolescence, he began living in an inner city area notorious for its homosexual activity. He engaged in a lifestyle of promiscuous homosexuality. As a young adult, he yielded his life to Jesus Christ as his Lord and Savior. Reading the book of Romans, he realized he would have to repent of his homosexual lifestyle. He underwent professional counseling in an effort to understand and overcome his homosexual tendencies.

Over the years, Dave gained a degree of accommodation to a celibate lifestyle. The temptation remains strong and he has stumbled more than once. But what has been harder for him than the struggle against temptation has been the struggle for acceptance. To this day he continues to search for a community of believers who will love him, affirm him, yet hold him accountable for the purity of his lifestyle. Tragically, such communities are all too rare. Dave once told me that the attitude he most frequently encounters in churches is, *"You change*—then we'll love you."

Dave needs to be accepted and loved *while* he is seeking to change. Until we in the church learn to practice Christlike unconditional acceptance, Dave and thousands like him will continue to be very lonely in their struggle for emotional transformation and wholeness.

I'm convinced of the truth of Romans 5:8—"God demonstrates His own love for us in this: While we were still sinners"—while we were still enemies of God—"Christ died for us." So if I cannot respond in a spirit of unconditional love toward *everyone*, regardless of how they differ from me, then the grace of God does not truly live in me. Because of the forgiveness God has shown me, His claim is on my life. God calls me to accept others in response to the grace and acceptance He has shown me.

In his book *Love, Acceptance and Forgiveness*, Jerry Cook tells of an incident that occurred in the church he pastors in northern Oregon. One day, he received a call from a friend of his, another pastor in town. Cook's friend was angry and emotional because Cook's church was growing and his own was not—in part because many of his own members had left to join the church Jerry Cook pastored. At one point this pastor said bitterly, "You know what you are in your church, Jerry? You're nothing but a bunch of garbage collectors!"

As Cook thought it over, he decided his friend— despite his heated irrationality—had a point. That's what we are in the church: garbage collectors. For what were we before Jesus found us? Just people who had been used up, cast aside, and forgotten. Then Jesus found us and "recycled" us, transformed us, and reshaped us for His own purpose.

A few Sundays later, Cook told this story in a sermon. Afterward, one of the members of the church came to him, grinning ear to ear. This man owned a trash collection company. "That's a terrific story you told this morning, Pastor," he beamed. "Let me tell you something about my business. There's a landfill near here that we've been filling with trash for the past ten years. Know what that landfill is today? A beautiful park."

Jerry Cook concludes, "I've seen human garbage become beautiful too. I've seen the stench of sin turned into the fragrance of heaven. That's our business . . . . When love, acceptance, and forgiveness prevail, the church of Jesus Christ becomes . . . a center of love designed for the healing of broken people, and a force for God."[2]

Let me pose a question to you: How high is your A.Q.? I'm not talking about your I.Q., your Intelligence Quotient. I'm asking about your *Acceptance* Quotient. How high and deep and broad is your A.Q. toward others in the church and in the world who are different from you? How's your A.Q. toward those who have fallen into sin?

How's your A.Q. toward that ex-pastor now disgraced by scandal?

How's your A.Q. toward that fellow church member who continually opposes your ideas and proposals?

How's your A.Q. toward people who have been through a divorce?

How's your A.Q. toward the young woman who has had an abortion?

How's your A.Q. toward those who are returning to church after drifting away from the faith and away from your friendship?

How's your A.Q. toward the embezzler, whose picture was on the front page of the newspaper last year?

How's your A.Q. toward the former prostitute who is coming off of drugs and now enters your church seeking a new start in life?

How is your A.Q. toward the unmarried teenager who has brought her baby into the nursery of your church?

How is our Acceptance Quotient? This is the test of whether the grace of God has truly penetrated your life and mine.

Perhaps you're a member of a growing church. You remember the tightly-knit little fellowship your church used to be. You remember when everyone in the church knew everyone else. You remember the days before the church began attracting so many *different* kinds of people—people of different denominational backgrounds or ministry styles or ethnic origin—and you're having a hard time accepting change, accepting new ministries, accepting new people. I recently came across a letter written by a woman who was in a similar situation. She writes:

> My husband and I are part of the "old guard." We helped found this church. We remember when our present church site was nothing but an orchard at the edge of town. We have fond memories of those days.
>
> Yet I have to say that we love these days of change and progress even more. Sure, we have to park blocks from church because the parking lot has gotten too small. Sometimes I have to put up with a stranger sitting in my lap during the third service, because there just isn't enough room for everyone who wants to worship here.
>
> But what's a little inconvenience compared with the thrill of seeing all these people gathered together, hungry to hear the Word of God being taught and applied? So what if we're packed together a little too close for comfort? I *love* it! And I wouldn't trade the excitement of these days for the nostalgia of the "good old days" in our tiny little church for anything!

Here is a woman who has learned, despite her fond memories of the past, to accept change and live in the now. Here is a woman with a high A.Q.

Tony Campolo tells a true story about the power of acceptance. It's the story of a school teacher named Miss Brown. She was a negative, critical, lonely woman without any family of her own. It was about twenty-five years ago that a little boy named Teddy came into Miss Brown's fifth-grade class. He was a friendless child just transferred from a school in another town.

To Miss Brown, Teddy seemed marked for failure. In fact, whenever Teddy did poorly on a test, Miss Brown would mark his paper with an extra-large F, as if she derived some sort of perverse satisfaction from singling him out as a failure.

Miss Brown hadn't bothered to check Teddy's school records, but if she had, she would have noticed the following notations: *First grade*—"Teddy shows promise, but comes from a difficult home situation." *Second grade*—"Teddy is a good boy, but too serious. His mother is terminally ill." *Third grade*—"Teddy cooperates, but he is detached. His mother died this year." *Fourth grade*—"Teddy is a slow learner. His father shows no interest in him." Clearly, there were reasons for Teddy's gradual slide toward failure that Miss Brown had never tried to understand.

At Christmastime, the boys and girls brought presents for their teacher. They sat in a circle and, one by one, Miss Brown opened her presents. At last she came to the present Teddy had brought, and when she unwrapped it she found a tarnished bracelet from which half the cut-glass stones were missing. Next to it was a half-empty bottle of cheap perfume. When the other children saw these second-hand gifts, they began to laugh.

For the first time since Teddy had come into her class, Miss Brown suddenly felt a twinge of pity for the boy. She immediately put the battered bracelet on her wrist and dabbed some of the cheap perfume on her neck and wrists. After class, when all the other children had gone home, Teddy came to Miss Brown and said, "Miss Brown, you smell just like my mother used to—before she died."

That night, Miss Brown had an encounter with Jesus Christ. She knelt beside her bed and begged God to forgive her for her bitter and unloving spirit. That was the beginning of a new relationship between Miss Brown and Teddy. From that day forward, she never failed to seek out and develop Teddy's true worth and abilities. This was the beginning of Teddy's transformation.

Over the years that followed, Teddy kept in touch with Miss Brown, sending her an occasional note. One read, in part:

Dear Miss Brown,
I wanted you to be the first to know. Next week I'll be graduating second in my high school class.

Love,
Teddy

A few years later, Teddy wrote:

Dear Miss Brown:
Just wanted to let you know I'll be graduating first in my class at the University. It was the hardest thing I've ever done, but it's also been the greatest experience of my life.

Love,
Teddy

Then this, several years later:

Dear Miss Brown,

I made it! As of today, I am Theodore J. Simmons, M.D. How about that? And one more thing: I'm going to be married on July 27th and I would be honored if you would come and sit where my mother would have sat. My Dad died last year and you're the only family I have now.

Love,
Teddy

Miss Brown went to Teddy's wedding and sat in the place of his mother. Today, Teddy is like a son to her, and his family is now her family. Liberated from her prison of loneliness, she now reaches out to others with the love of Jesus Christ. When she unleashed her own Acceptance Quotient toward a lonely little boy, she experienced healing from her own loneliness. Most important of all, she discovered the truth of Paul's message in Romans 15: "Accept one another, then, just as Christ accepted you, in order to bring praise to God."

How is your A.Q.?

Chapter 18

Affectionately Yours, Paul
(Romans 16)

Our daughter, Rachael, was born more than two and a half months prematurely, weighing only three pounds. Within a few days, her weight dropped even further. She developed a serious lung problem called hyaline membrane disease, along with other complications. She spent the first six weeks of her life in an incubator in Children's Hospital in downtown Minneapolis.

The incubator had openings through which Shirley and I could put our hands so we could stroke her arms and legs. Hour after hour, we sat beside our daughter, touching and soothing her, helping her to feel our presence as she struggled for life.

After she was released from the hospital, we took Rachael home. There, on doctors' orders, she spent the first year of her life in isolation from all contact with people except Shirley and me. The condition of her lungs was so precarious that not even other relatives were allowed near her, lest she catch some stray virus. Since Rachael's contact with other people was necessarily limited, Shirley and I made sure to give our little Rachael a lot of holding, stroking, and hugging during that year.

Today Rachael is a happy, healthy teenager. In the years since she was born, I've learned a lot about the importance of physical touch, of demonstrated affection, in the lives of little children—and in the lives of grownups.

Diane Ackerman, author of *A Natural History of the Senses*, cites studies by author Saul Schanberg at Duke University and Dr. Tiffany Field at the University of Miami Medical School that show the importance of touch for premature infants. Many of the parents whose infants were observed in these studies were unable to give time and affection to their premature child because of stress, emotional problems, job pressures, drug or alcohol addiction, ignorance, or indifference.

The studies showed that babies who received fifteen minutes of gentle massage three times a day experienced forty-seven percent faster weight gain than babies left alone in their incubators (and weight gain, of course, is a crucial factor in infant survival rates). Researchers also concluded that massaged babies were more active, more alert and more responsive to people and rattles. Their nervous systems matured more rapidly than those of untouched babies. They were discharged from the hospital an average of six days earlier than untouched babies. At eight months of age, touched babies tested noticeably higher in mental and motor ability than untouched babies.

"The policy with premature babies used to be not to disturb them any more than necessary," Ackerman concludes. "They lived in a kind of isolation booth. But now the evidence about touch is so plentiful and eloquent that more hospitals are encouraging large-scale touching . . . . Vitamin T, for Touch, seems to be as essential as sunlight."[1]

A similar phenomenon is reported by missionary nurses and doctors in starvation-plagued regions such as

India, Southeast Asia, and parts of Africa. Starving babies need more than milk to survive. If they are held, cuddled, and stroked as they are fed, they generally live. If not, they usually die—even if they receive the same amount and quality of food and medicine.

Just as demonstrated affection is crucial to the life of a child, Paul in Romans 16 affirms that affection is a key ingredient in the life of the church. In fact, Paul has been affirming the crucial importance of affection throughout his letter to the Romans. In chapter 1, he expresses his own affection for the Christians in Rome, writing, "I remember you in my prayers at all times . . . . I long to see you . . . ." In chapter 12, he says, "Love must be sincere . . . . Be devoted to one another in brotherly love."

Notice, incidentally, that the English phrase "brotherly love" in Romans 12:10 is not the best translation. In the original Greek, it conveys a sense of "family-like affection." So what Paul is really saying to the church is, "Be affectionately devoted to the other members of your church family as if they were your parents, your brothers and sisters, or your own children."

In Romans 16, we come to Paul's postscript, his personal love-note appended to the end of his theological masterpiece. The theme of this chapter is *affection*, and every line brims with encouragement and remembrance for those who have been his friends, his mentors, his disciples, his partners in ministry. In this chapter, Paul mentions thirty-five people by name. I'm sure that not one of those thirty-five people ever imagined his or her name would be immortalized in the pages of Holy Scriptures, to be read and studied by generations of believers for the next two thousand years.

It would be easy to simply skip over this postscript with its long list of names and say, "Well, I guess we've pretty well covered the book of Romans. Oh, there's one last chapter, but it just reads like a telephone book." In fact, if you go to your church library or Christian bookstore and search the commentaries on Romans, you'll find that the majority of them—including the commentaries of such theologians as John Calvin, Martin Luther, and Karl Barth—give Romans 16 little more than a passing glance.

Yet Romans 16 is the key to understanding the true character of the early Christian church. Reading between the lines of this chapter, we can see how fluid and mobile the early church was. The people he greets by name are believers from far-flung regions of the then-known world—Italy, Greece, Asia, Palestine, perhaps even Persia. In Romans 16, we also see how culturally and ethnically diverse the early church was. And, too, we see how affectionate and caring the early church was.

Despite the richness of this chapter, Romans 16 remains the most ignored chapter in the New Testament. On one level this is understandable. But on another level, this is absolutely tragic, for so much of the apostle Paul's heart and life is embedded here in Romans 16. Indeed, I submit to you that it is here, in the final chapter of Romans, that we see in a practical, dynamic way how the powerful truths of the first 15 chapters of Romans are to be lived out.

One important fact that emerges from even a cursory glance at the chapter is that Paul knew people by name. He had spent time with them and had invested his life in them. The depth of Paul's relationships is etched into the page.

In Romans 1, Paul says that he has wanted to visit the believers in Rome before this, but has not been able to. A question occurs: If Paul has never visited the church in Rome, how is it he knows so many people there? Answer: Because the people he greets at the end of this letter are people he has worked with in Greece, in Asia Minor, in Palestine. They were his partners in ministry, they trained under him and learned from him, and then he sent them out in ministry, and many of them settled in Rome to help establish the church there.

Implicit in this passage is a key principle of Paul's life: More time spent with fewer individuals results in greater lasting impact for Christ. Though Paul was a gifted pastor, teacher, preacher, and evangelist, he did not spend the bulk of his time in ministry preaching to the masses. He spent most of the time pouring his life into individual people.

Not long ago, I was visited in my office by Charles R. Swindoll, the gifted author, radio teacher, and pastor of the First Evangelical Free Church of Fullerton, California. He brought with him two young men who were serving an internship on the staff of his church. Chuck and his two friends were traveling up and down the West Coast, visiting different churches, meeting with pastors, and studying how different churches approached ministry and worship. I was impressed by the fact that Chuck Swindoll—a man who is in demand to address crowds of ten and fifteen thousand at a time—would take the time to invest his life in these two interns. At the end of a year, those two young men will leave the Fullerton church—but they will take with them something of Chuck Swindoll.

I was impressed—but not surprised. For Chuck Swindoll is simply patterning his own ministry after that of Jesus, who poured His life into the twelve, and after that of Paul, who poured his life into many of the thirty-five people listed in Romans 16. Paul lists these people by name because he knows them, he has served with them, he has affection for them.

Another key fact that emerges from a study of Romans 16 is the profoundly important role of women in the early church. This passage is one of many that counter the lie now in vogue that accuses Christianity of historically oppressing and downgrading women. The truth is that it is Jesus Christ and the faith He founded that elevated women to a place they never before enjoyed in human history. In fact, I firmly believe that the advances and equality that women have achieved in recent decades would have been impossible without the ideals of just, ethical, equal treatment Christianity imparted to our society.

In Romans 16, we see that Paul affirms the key leadership role women have played in the spread of the Christian gospel. Here are just a few examples:

Verses 1 and 2: "I commend to you our sister Phoebe, a servant of the church in Cenchrea . . . . She has been a great help to many people, including me." Phoebe was probably a deaconess in the church in Cenchrea, a city near Corinth in southern Greece. It was she who risked her life to carry Paul's letter to Rome. Phoebe probably had the spiritual gift of helping, for it seems she performed a role of helping and supporting Paul in ministry so that he could be free to effectively use his gifts. Perhaps she fixed meals and ran errands for Paul and other apostles. Perhaps she even tended his wounds and mended his clothes after he was beaten or stoned. We can only speculate on the exact nature of her role as a helper to Paul.

What we can say for sure about Phoebe is that she serves as a model for so many in the church today who, in quiet and frequently unseen ways, minister for the cause of the Christian gospel. Every effective church has its Phoebes, and without people like Phoebe there would be no dynamic, thriving churches. I suspect we will one day be surprised to discover the high place of honor God has reserved in heaven for Phoebe and her kind—humble Christian servants who exercise the gift of helping without any desire for recognition or applause.

Verse 3: "Greet Priscilla and Aquila, my fellow workers in Christ Jesus." The story of Priscilla and her husband Aquila is recorded in Acts 18. They opened their home to Paul, allowing him to live with them for a year and a half. They went with Paul to Ephesus, where they had an effective mentoring relationship with a young believer named Apollos. Apollos later became one of the pillars of the early church, and had an important role in establishing the church at Corinth. As Paul wrote of the Corinthian church, "I planted the seed, Apollos watered it, but God made it grow." Priscilla and Aquila were vital links in a chain of discipleship: Paul discipled them; they discipled Apollos; Apollos "watered the seed" in Corinth; and the ministry of the gospel multiplied.

Verse 7: "Greet Andronicus and Junias, my relatives who have been in prison with me. They are outstanding among the apostles, and they were in Christ before I was." Most scholars agree that Junias is a feminine name, and tend to view Andronicus and Junias as another husband-wife team. Paul pays them a special honor, calling them "outstanding among the apostles." The fact that they have been in prison with Paul and that their conversion to Christ predates Paul's attests to the level of their courage, commitment, and Christian maturity.

Verse 12: "Greet Tryphena and Tryphosa, those women who work hard in the Lord." Most Bible scholars agree that these two are sisters—perhaps even twins, given the similarity of their names—who were in ministry together for Jesus Christ.

Again, verse 12: "Greet my dear friend Persis, another woman who has worked very hard in the Lord." The name *Persis* literally means *Persian woman*. The phrase "worked very hard" is a weak translation of a Greek phrase that could more accurately be rendered "worked to the point of exhaustion."

And the list goes on: Verse 6 mentions Mary, one of six Marys mentioned in the New Testament. Verse 13 mentions the mother of Rufus. Verse 15 mentions Julia, plus an unnamed sister of Nereus. Clearly, women held a key role of leadership and ministry in the early church. Nowhere in these lines is there the least hint that women were treated as second-class citizens of the kingdom of God.

Verse 16 brings us to the heart of this chapter, and the heart of the apostle Paul. He tells the believers in Rome, "Greet one another with a holy kiss." How quickly our culturally biased eyes scan past that line!

But let me tell you about a man who takes Romans 16:16 seriously. He is my friend Ray Stedman, who has been pastor of Peninsula Bible Church in Palo Alto for the past forty years. You probably know him for his books, *Body Life*, *Authentic Christianity*, or his excellent two-volume commentary on Romans, *From Guilt to Glory*. I've known Ray for many years, and he has become one of my mentors. I consider him a mentor in my life not only because of his years of experience as a Christian teacher, nor merely because of his great wisdom and discernment. I look to him as a mentor in large measure because of his genuine demonstration of Christian affection.

Whenever Ray and I meet at church or at the airport, he hugs me and unabashedly kisses me on the neck: a holy kiss. The same thing happens when we say good-bye. This kind of holy affection is rare in the church of the 1990s. It is a sadly neglected part of our biblical heritage. I'm grateful to Ray for boldly keeping alive the practice of godly Christian affection.

Another man who demonstrated such affection was my brother, Paul. This big, athletically-built coach was not afraid, whenever we would see each other after an absence (he lived in Denver while I lived on the West Coast), to give me a hug and a kiss on the neck, man to man.

One of the many tragic consequences of our society's confusion over the issue of homosexuality is our pervasive cultural fear of the demonstration of affection man to man, father to son, two men with their arms around each other, two men embracing. If you have traveled in other countries and experienced other cultures, then you may have observed that this fear of demonstrating affection is not the norm throughout the rest of the world. For example, throughout Latin America—where Latin men jealously guard their rugged macho image—it's not unusual for men to greet one another or say good-bye to one another with an *abrazo*, an embrace.

I saw this same unreserved demonstration of man-to-man affection among the Christians I met in Ethiopia. These believers were knit tightly together by persecution and hardship, for they were daily risking their lives for Jesus Christ in a fiercely Marxist country. Some had spent several harrowing months in prison for the "crime" of telling others about Jesus. Upon their release from prison, they greeted each other with an embrace and a holy kiss. And they didn't reserve their godly affection only for each other. They also demonstrated affection toward strangers. When my traveling companion and I stepped out of our four-wheel-drive vehicles and onto the dusty streets of their village, these Ethiopian believers rushed up to us, hugged us, kissed us on the neck, and said, "I love you."

In our western culture, we need to re-learn what many people in other cultures have never forgotten: the importance of showing affection. We need to re-learn it in our churches and we need to re-learn it in our families.

Some time ago, author-evangelist Leighton Ford and his wife were interviewed on the *Focus on the Family* radio program. They were discussing the death of their son Sandy and how they worked through their grief. The essential conclusion of Leighton Ford's message was this: "We hurt deeply over the loss of our son, but I'm grateful that we had the kind of relationship with Sandy that allowed us to give him back to God without regrets. The parents we really hurt for are those who bear the guilt and regret of never having demonstrated affection to their children. When their children leave home or die, there are no more chances to say, 'I love you.'"

I recently read about just this kind of father, the kind who will have no more chances to demonstrate affection to his son. On his fiftieth birthday, this father was in his easy chair after a hard day at work. His eleven-year-old son bounced into the room and leaped into his father's lap. He wrapped his arms around his father's neck and began kissing his father on the cheek.

"What are you doing?" the father said in annoyance. He just wanted to read his paper. He didn't want to be bothered.

"Today's your birthday, Dad!" said the boy. "I'm going to give you fifty kisses, one for every year!"

"Not now," grumbled the father, pushing his son from his lap. "Maybe later. Just get off me!"

The boy walked out of the house, and the father continued reading his paper. Outside, the boy climbed on his bicycle and rode off down the block. Three blocks from home he was struck and killed by a car.

I don't ever want to suffer the guilt and remorse this father must bear. I want to know that, no matter what happens in this life, the last words I imparted to my children were words of affection, not words of indifference or rejection. Even after my children leave my presence— when they go to school, when they go to a soccer game, when they stay overnight with a friend— I want them to still feel the touch of my love, and the lingering warmth of my arms around them.

In his book, *How To Really Love Your Child*, Christian psychiatrist Ross Campbell observes that the three most important ways of demonstrating love to our children are focused attention, eye contact, and physical contact. Tragically, most fathers are increasingly reluctant to demonstrate affection for their children by touching, hugging, or kissing them. This is due in part to increased self-consciousness in the wake of increased publicity of molestation and incest cases. Many fathers are afraid that by showing physical affection to their sons they will feminize them and turn them toward homosexuality (when in fact, the opposite is true). And many fathers are simply so busy and self-involved they have little time or emotional energy to give their children.

Affectionate physical contact between parents and their children is a key factor in a child's emotional and psychological well-being. In boys, the need for physically demonstrated affection is strongest in the earliest years, tapering off (though never disappearing completely) as a boy approaches adolescence. In girls, the need for physical affection increases from early childhood on, and actually peaks at around age twelve. Yet, despite the crucial importance of physical affection in the life of a growing child, most children simply do not get the emotional nourishment they need from their parents, especially from their fathers.

Campbell tells about a friend of his named Rusty, a tough-as-nails Marine drill instructor with four sons. Rusty wanted his boys to be like him, rugged and masculine, so he treated his boys like Marine recruits. He offered them no affection, no hugs, only stern military discipline and emotional distance. "The last time I saw these boys," Campbell concludes, "each one was extremely effeminate. Their mannerisms, speech, and appearance were those of girls. Surprised? You shouldn't be. I see it every day. Boys with rejecting, harsh, non-affectionate fathers generally become effeminate."[2] In our families, as in our churches, we need to re-learn the ministry of an affectionate embrace, of a holy kiss.

What is the origin of the holy kiss Paul encourages in Romans 16:16? To understand what Paul is saying, we have to understand something of the background of the early church in Rome. This church went through persecution and suffering beyond what you and I can imagine. As a result of this persecution, the church went underground—not metaphorically "underground" as we use the term today, but *literally* underground. The church met in the catacombs, subterranean burial galleries composed of tunnels, niches, and chambers. The church also met in the homes of believers, often changing locations from one home to the next to avoid government detection.

If you were a first-century Christian in Rome, you would meet with your small group of believers in a home or in the catacombs one week. Then, the next time you met, you would find your group a little smaller, because during the week one or two members, or perhaps a whole family, had been taken away by Nero's soldiers. You might miss members of your immediate family—your husband, your child, your sister, your father. So early Christians lived with enormous uncertainty about the future.

When they gathered for worship, they always celebrated a meal together. At the end of each meal, these early Christians would set aside a portion of the bread and wine for the "love feast," the celebration of holy communion. It was not something they did as a mere ritual. Rather, it was an act of intimate fellowship with God and with one another in the body of Christ.

After the "love feast," it was time for the group of believers to disperse. But they didn't dare leave all at once, or some unfriendly observer might alert the authorities that secret meetings were taking place. So these Christians would slip away from the house or the catacombs, one or two at a time. Before they left each other, they hugged, a powerful non-verbal expression of their mutual love. It was as if they were saying, "I may never see you again in this life. But I want you to know I love you. I'll pray for you. If the soldiers come and take me to my death, I'll be waiting for you in heaven."

Then one last expression of their godly affection before parting: They would kiss each other on the left side of the neck, then on the right side. A holy kiss.

Years passed. Persecution waned. The underground church went above ground and became prosperous. The open demonstration of affection gradually declined. The "love feast" ceased to be a communal meal. It became an institutional service. Even though the sacrament of communion remains an important and overwhelmingly meaningful aspect of Christian worship, it is rarely practiced anymore with the kind of family-like intimacy it once entailed. The embrace that used to conclude first-century Christian worship disappeared. The holy kiss between believers was replaced by a kiss on the forehead by a priest as the believer received the sacrament of communion.

More time passed. The priest no longer kissed the believer's forehead during communion. Instead, he kissed the believer's hand. More time passed, and the kiss was removed from the believer altogether. Now the priest kissed an object rather than a person. He kissed the cup or a scroll containing some holy words or a stole, a band of cloth that the priest himself wore over his shoulders.

Do you see what has happened in the history of the church since the time of Paul? The affection God intended us to show one another in the body of Christ has gradually been transferred from *people* to *things*. This, in fact, is a parable of what has taken place in our lives. If we are honest, we have to confess that our own affection is all too easily transferred from people to such things as careers, homes, and financial investments.

Paul says, "Greet one another with a holy kiss." Yet as we pass through our houses of worship Sunday after Sunday, we rub shoulders with men and women who are hurting, lonely, and broken. They don't need our pity or our advice or our money. They just need someone to reach out and embrace them, to love them, to say, "I care about you." They need someone to greet them with a holy kiss. They need the touch of godly affection. You may protest that such affection needs to be done in an appropriate way. My answer would be, "Yes, *but it needs to be done.*"

How are we living out the counsel of Romans 16 in our churches at the end of the twentieth century? Are we reaching out to the lonely and hurting people in our own fellowship? Are we watchful for opportunities to meet and greet newcomers so we can draw them into the warmth of our fellowship? Are we looking for ways to demonstrate affection to the lonely and elderly in our fellowship?

I'll never forget Eleanor, a widow in her eighties, whom I greeted at the door after one Sunday church service. She reached out to shake my hand, but I felt compelled to do more than simply return her handshake. I hugged her and gave her a kiss on the cheek. She hugged me back, then placed her hands on my shoulders and said, "Thank you, Ron. When you hugged me just now, and when we joined hands and sang a praise chorus during the service—well, those are the only times anyone ever touches me anymore. It means more to me than you know." Paul said, "Greet one another with a holy kiss." His counsel is as relevant in the 1990s as it was when the ink on the page was still fresh.

Jacob Lowen tells the true story of two seven-year-old boys, Billy and Jim. Billy was a Christian, and he had a burden for his friend Jim. He wanted to find some way to introduce Jim to Jesus Christ as Lord and Savior.

One day, a terrible tragedy came into Jim's life: His father was killed in a tractor accident. A few days later Billy encountered his friend Jim at school. Jim was alone, walking alongside one of the school buildings, his feet shuffling, his eyes downcast.

"How are you, Jim?" asked Billy.

"Fine," said Jim. His feet continued shuffling. His eyes remained downcast.

Billy knew everything was far from "fine" in Jim's life. He wanted to say something to comfort his friend, but he didn't know what to say. On an impulse, he reached out to Jim and hugged him without a word.

Then Jim took Billy's arm and led him around the corner of the building. "I'm not really fine, Billy. I miss my dad. And my mom cries all day. The farm machinery is broken down and it looks like my mom is going to lose the farm. I'm not fine at all, and until you hugged me, I didn't think anyone in this school even cared."

Shortly afterward, Billy shared his faith in Jesus with Jim, and Jim received Jesus Christ as his Lord and Savior. Today, Jim is a grown man, serving God in full-time Christian ministry. Billy had actually loved his friend Jim into the kingdom of God through a demonstration of affection.

In Romans 12, Paul tells us to love each other with a genuine love, to hate what is evil, to hold fast to what is good. He tells us to love one another in the church with a devoted, family-like affection. Then, in Romans 16, Paul gives us a practical demonstration of Christian affection, showing us by his example how our Christian love is to work itself out in the church. To some people this chapter reads like a telephone book, but to me it is the most fitting and perfect ending imaginable to the greatest letter ever written. For between the lines, you can almost see these words in that bold, large-lettered scrawl that was Paul's trademark:

Affectionately yours,
Paul

FOOTNOTES

Chapter 1

[1] Tacitus, *The Annals*, Great Books of the Western World, vol. 15 (Chicago: Encyclopædia Britannica, 1952), p. 166.

[2] Tacitus, p. 168.

[3] Earl F. Palmer, *Salvation by Surprise* (Waco, TX: Word, 1975), pp. 11–12.

[4] Saint Augustine, *The Confessions; The City of God; On Christian Doctrine*, Great Books of the Western World, vol. 18 (Chicago: Encyclopædia Britannica, 1952), p. 9.

[5] Saint Augustine, pp. 60–61.

Chapter 2

[1] Ron Lee Davis, *A Forgiving God in an Unforgiving World* (Eugene, OR: Harvest House, 1984), p. 53.

Chapter 3

[1] Robert Jastrow, *God and the Astronomers* (New York: Norton, 1978), p. 12.

[2] Jastrow, p. 14.

[3] C. S. Lewis, *Mere Christianity* (New York: Macmillan, 1960), p. 19.

[4] Alan Hayward, *God Is* (Nashville: Nelson, 1978), p. 172.

[5] Jerry Cook with Stanley C. Baldwin, *Love, Acceptance and Forgiveness* (Ventura, CA: Regal, 1979), pp. 69–70.

Chapter 4
[1] C. S. Lewis, *Mere Christianity* (New York: Macmillan, 1960), pp. 94–95.

Chapter 5
[1] Frederick Pohl, *The Way the Future Was* (New York: Del Rey/Ballantine, 1978), pp. 14–15.
[2] C. S. Lewis, *The Weight of Glory* (New York: Macmillan, 1949), pp. 14–15.

Chapter 6
[1] Alvin Toffler, *The Third Wave* (New York: Morrow, 1980), p. 391.
[2] C. S. Lewis, *The Screwtape Letters* (New York: Macmillan, 1943), p. 70.

Chapter 8
[1] F. B. Meyer, Joseph (Fort Worth, PA: CLC, n.d.), p. 30.
[2] Cal Thomas (interview), "Moral Failures and Small Groups." *Discipleship Journal*, September 1987, p. 42.

Chapter 9
[1] Edith Pendleton, ed., *Too Old to Cry . . . Too Young to Die* (Nashville: Nelson, 1980), p. 34.

Chapter 10
[1] Fritz Ridenour, *How to be a Christian Without Being Religious* (Glendale, CA. Regal Books, G/L Publications, 1967), p. 74.

Chapter 11
[1] Ray C. Stedman, *From Guilt to Glory*, vol. 2 (Portland, OR: Multnomah, 1985), p. 52.

Chapter 12

[1] Source: A 1978 study by R. Illsley and M. Hall (see *Abortion in Psychosocial Perspective* [New York: Springer, 1978], pp. 11–21). Other studies suggest the figure may even be less than one percent.

[2] Matthew 10:39, Mark 8:35, Luke 9:24, and John 12:25.

Chapter 13

[1] In the original Greek, this word has a primary connotation of "telling forth" and only a secondary connotation of "foretelling" or predicting future events.

[2] I would underscore the word *cheerful* with regard to the gift of giving. The person who uses his material donations as a means of getting his way or controlling the ministry of a church either does not possess the spiritual gift of giving, or disobediently resists using his spiritual gift in the cheerful, no-strings attached manner that God intended. See Romans 12:8, 2 Corinthians 9:7, and 1 Timothy 6:17–18.

[3] Obviously, every Christian is expected to have faith. However, God gives to some Christians a special and extraordinary gift of faith. Many of the spiritual gifts listed in the Bible (such as encouraging, giving, mercy, service, wisdom, faith, discernment, evangelism, and intercessory prayer) are qualities that *all* Christians are expected to display in some measure, but that *some* Christians receive in extra measure.

Chapter 17

[1] Elton Trueblood, *The Company of the Committed*, (New York: Harper and Row, 1961), pp. 96 and 98.

[2] Jerry Cook with Stanley C. Baldwin, *Love, Acceptance and Forgiveness* (Ventura, CA: Regal, 1979), p. 22.

Chapter 18
[1]Diane Ackerman, "The Power of Touch," *Parade Magazine*, March 25, 1990, p. 5.
[2]Ross Campbell, *How To Really Love Your Child* (Wheaton, IL: Victor, 1979), p. 72.

ACKNOWLEDGMENTS

I have been teaching *Paul's Letter to the Romans* for the past twenty years to various groups of people throughout the United States and overseas. My deep affection and high regard for this brilliant theological treatise has only deepened with each passing year. Therefore, it is a dream come true for me to see this book become a reality. A number of my friends have contributed to the process of publishing *Becoming a Whole Person in a Broken World*, and I want to express my deep gratitude to each one.

My friend and brother in Christ, Jim Denney, has tirelessly researched, refined, developed, and edited the material contained in this work. His efforts are obvious on every page and there would have been no book without him. This is the seventh book Jim and I have collaborated on together and my regard for him grows with each new publication and each passing year.

Helen McKinney, my gifted administrative assistant and dear friend, has carefully critiqued each chapter of this book and has been a constant source of encouragement to Jim Denney, to our friends at Discovery House Publishers, and to me throughout this process. Helen is a special gift given by God's grace to assist me in the many facets of my ministry.

It was only through the constant encouragement of my friend, Bob DeVries, publisher for Discovery House Publishers, that this book has become a reality. Bob is a winsome Christian with a sincere love for God and His

Word. It's a joy to work with an editor who genuinely seeks to enable others to grow in their walk with God.

Joan Callahan, a special sister in Christ, has spent many hours organizing various material and illustrations from my messages so that I could more readily adapt their insights into this book.

Most importantly, my wife, Shirley, and our children, Rachael and Nathan, have been extremely supportive of this project and have continually encouraged me through the lengthy process of writing this book.

As always, I'm especially thankful to the scores of friends who have shared their lives with me so the truth of Romans can be given contemporary application. The transparency and vulnerability of so many friends has helped me to better understand how God's Word is so practical and applicable for our lives today. I am deeply grateful to each one of them.

Note to the Reader

The publisher invites you to share your response to the message of this book by writing Discovery House Publishers, P.O. Box 3566, Grand Rapids, MI 49501, U.S.A. or by calling 1-800-283-8333. For information about other Discovery House publications, contact us at the same address and phone number.